Great Old-Fashioned American Recipes

◆

Also by Beatrice Ojakangas

Great Old-Fashioned American Desserts

The Great Holiday Baking Book

The Great Scandinavian Baking Book

Great Whole Grain Breads

Scandinavian Feasts

Scandinavian Cooking

Quick Breads

Pot Pies

Great
Old-Fashioned
◆ American ◆
Recipes

Beatrice Ojakangas

University of Minnesota Press
Minneapolis • London

For Mom and Lisa

Illustrations by Mark Tucci
Copyright 1988 by HPBooks

Originally published by HPBooks, 1988
First University of Minnesota Press edition, 2005

Published by the University of Minnesota Press
111 Third Avenue South, Suite 290
Minneapolis, MN 55401-2520
http://www.upress.umn.edu

Library of Congress Cataloging-in-Publication Data

Ojakangas, Beatrice A.
    [Country tastes]
    Great old-fashioned American recipes / Beatrice Ojakangas.
        p.   cm.
    Originally published as: Country tastes : best recipes from America's kitchens, 1988.
    Includes index.
    ISBN 0-8166-4810-7 (pb : alk. paper)
    1. Cookery, American.   I. Title.
    TX715.O413 2005
    641.5973—dc22

                                                                          2005018042

Printed in the United States of America on acid-free paper

The University of Minnesota is an equal-opportunity educator and employer.

14 13 12 11 10 09 08 07 06 05   10 9 8 7 6 5 4 3 2 1

CONTENTS

ACKNOWLEDGMENTS

When I write a cookbook, everybody around me gets involved. Luckily, my surroundings contain my support group. I want to thank my family and friends for help and encouragement to complete this book. These include my parents, Esther and Ted Luoma, my nine brothers and sisters, Leonard, Marion, Lillian, Betty Mae, Rudy, Eugene, Nancy, Alvin, and Dawn. Much gratitude also to my immediate family, Dick, Cathy, Greg, and Susanna, and to my parents-in-law, Grace and Earl Wold.

Friends play an important role, especially those who will happily "test" recipes, as is the case with the members of the Sarah Circle of First Lutheran Church. Thanks for the two "December" testings to Marj Bergeland, Peggy Cooke, Chris Coyner, Rose Drewes, Kay Eckman, Diane Ellison, Helen Gildseth, Sharlene Hensrud, Mary Holt, Jeannette Huntley, Lois Jaeckel, Nancy Lokken, Marcia Lothner, Jean McKinnon, Avis Opheim, Brenda Sproat, Annette Stevens, Beth Storaasli, Norma Jean Strommen, Joanadelle Tetlie, Jean Elton Turbes, and Gudrun Witrack.

In addition, I would like to express my gratitude to professional friends for their ideas, help, and encouragement. Thanks to Arlene Wanderman and Howard Helmer at Food Communications in New York and to the home economists at General Foods, General Mills, and Pillsbury Mills.

I wish to acknowledge the help of the Duluth Public Library and staff, who willingly researched answers to off-the-wall historical questions about early America.

Thanks, too, to my friendly editor, Roni Durie, who has been so great to work with, and Jeanette Egan at HPBooks. I count both as friends and coworkers.

WHAT IS AMERICAN COUNTRY COOKING?

♦

American country cooking is a story of cows and chickens and barnyard animals, of wild berries and fruits and vegetables. Although it may be a picture we have of our own growing-up years, there are still farm kitchens that spill over at times with eggs and milk, or tomatoes, green beans and other garden abundance. The kitchen turns into a factory in the summertime as the rhubarb is ready, the strawberries ripen, the cucumbers and zucchini proliferate.

This seasonal abundance birthed the idea of festivals. Apple festivals were probably the prototype and began in the 1800's when coun-

try folk discovered that the tedium of paring and slicing apples could be broken by community effort. Festivals today celebrate the abundance of everything from catfish to dates, seafood, mushrooms, chickens, tomatoes, asparagus, strawberries, blueberries, wild rice, watermelon, rhubarb, cherries, pumpkins, zucchini, hot chiles, okra, pecans, cranberries and even garlic! They are more an excuse for a community party than to do any real work.

American country cooking has been a story of ingenuity and "making do." When the right ingredient was not there, it was either elimi-

ated or a substitute found. Country cooking is simple and honest and touched with nostalgia, a bit of ethnicity, regionality and history.

The American country scene pictures a cool, refreshing glass of iced tea in a small town on a hot, lazy, summer day. It's kids selling lemonade on the corner. It's also a cup of steaming coffee at 40 below zero shared in a small town café over sweet rolls by farmers in buffalo-check wool shirts and bib overalls. It's the stew and apple pie that awaits at home. It's the loaf cakes, breads, cheese and cookies that are there to snack on. Country cooking includes meat loaves, chicken pies and cole slaw, freshly baked breads, pies and shortcakes. It is tamale pie, cowboy steak, hangtown fry, chicken and biscuits, mulligan stew, clam chowder, pumpkin soup, or meatballs in cream gravy.

Country cooking recalls the first Thanksgiving as we relish the aroma of stuffed turkey in the oven and pumpkin pies cooling, and sing hymns of thankfulness. It also makes us remember all that we have learned from each other's heritage and from the bounty shared by the Native American Indians who were the first cooking teachers on this side of the Atlantic.

Our Statue of Liberty makes this invitation:
". . . Give me your tired, your poor,
your huddled masses, yearning to
breathe free—the wretched refuse
of your teeming shore. Send these,
the homeless, tempest and tos't to
me. I lift my lamp beside the golden
door." (Emma Lazarus).

Our ancestors came from teeming shores. You'd think we would be a nation of lame

ducks. Rather, we are a country of survivors. Our immigrant grandparents may have been poor and wretched, but they did not arrive empty-handed. They brought with them their taste for their native cuisine, their cookery skills, and their adaptability to use new and unfamiliar grains, fruits, vegetables and meats in dishes that reflect what was familiar to them. This has resulted in an American "foreign" cuisine of dishes that are non-existant in the "old country." Swiss steak cannot be found in Switzerland or Russian dressing in the U.S.S.R. Try to get French dressing in France or cioppino in Italy! The Chinese consider chop suey and chow mein "peculiar American hash."

To read the menu of country cooking across America has some similarity to reading your own telephone book. Ours in Duluth, population of about 90,000, ranges from Aaberg, to Franckowiak, to five pages of Johnsons, to Pierret, to Rauschenfels, to Ylitalo to Zywot, with hardly an ethnic group that is not represented in between.

The big migration from Europe was in the century between 1820 and 1920 when 33 million emigrated to America. Eighty percent of these people came from nine countries, Germany, Ireland, Italy, Austria, Russia, Great Britain, Norway, Denmark and France. The remaining 20 percent came from many other countries.

It has often been said that America is a "melting pot," as if we were all put together into some kind of cream soup. Rather, we are more like a colorful stew to which we all add our own color and texture to learn and share with each other, so that while we blend together, we also retain our own identity.

Good cooking depends on what the country has to offer. The fanciest of restaurants still depends on food grown on farms. We are not talking about "fancy" cuisine in this book. I remember as a girl reading about hors d'oeuvres and canapés and all kinds of fancy pastries and wondering when you'd ever serve those things. Like exotic dress, there wasn't the occasion for such "exotic" fare on the farm. Instead of being inventive, in this book we are concentrating on dishes that in some way reflect many parts of the country and many different cuisines. But, each recipe has been tested and reworked to make it easy to prepare with today's ingredients. In many cases, the recipe that originally served a large number, is worked down so it now serves four to six.

There was when I grew up, and may still be, one distinctive difference between "country" and "city" meals. It was what they were called. In the city, they were called breakfast, lunch and dinner. In the country, it was breakfast, dinner and supper. "Lunch" was what you had any other time, like in the middle of the afternoon, or after an evening meeting or event. Or, even after a wedding or a funeral.

This collection is in no way complete. It can never be. It is a selection of recipes and stories biased by my own interests and those around me in this time and this place.

BEEF

"I am an eater of beef." said Shakespeare. This he had in common with Midwestern and Western cattle farmers, as well as with most Americans. American country custom has traditionally spotlighted a platter of meat carried to the table for just about every meal. Beef has been, probably always will be, the favorite meat on the American table. Its simple abundance is what accounts for its dominance.

Beef cattle were raised on Southern farms before the Civil War. The war devastated the livestock in the South, but longhorn cattle had been trailed into Texas. Here they proliferated to the point where beef was so inexpensive that it was said a cow could be raised as cheaply as a chicken in any other part of the country.

Between 1870 and 1890, 10 million steers were driven by cowboys along the old "Chisholm Trail" from San Antonio to Abilene, Kansas. The cross-country railroad had reached Abilene by 1867. From there the cattle were shipped live to Eastern markets.

Cincinnati became the first meat-packing city because of its location on the Ohio river and its accessibility to the railroad. Cured meats were shipped downstream to Southern markets.

The center of the meat-packing industry shifted to Chicago when Gustavus Franklin Swift who had started in the meat business in Boston, moved his operations to Chicago. By 1875 he had built the earliest refrigerated railroad cars by packing them with ice at both ends. Swift was the first to ship dressed meats to the Eastern markets. P.D. Armour moved to Chicago at about the same time, but shipped only live cattle.

Old-fashioned beef recipes include a lot of pot roasts, simmered stews and ground-beef recipes which are still favorites with Americans and have been adapted to the tastes of particular ethnic backgrounds.

For the hearty Sunday meal, early roasts were hung in the fireplace on a hemp string and turned by hand as they roasted. Sometimes the string was twisted tight and allowed to turn by itself until it stopped, then it was twisted again. The cook's life was made a little easier with the invention of a clockwork-type band which was suspended from the fireplace and used to make the meat turn.

Swedish Meatballs

— ◆ —

A Swedish friend once told me that she inherited through her mother her grandmother's original can of ground pepper! And it was still half-full because pepper was a spice rarely used in everyday cooking which included such standbys as meatballs. Basic meatballs are still one of the most often served form for ground beef, be it a weekday supper, a Sunday "dinner," or "lunch" after a wedding. They are usually served with a simple sour-cream gravy, but the increasing use of American-style barbecue sauce shows the blending of two authentic tastes. Meatballs are often shaped and fried in butter the old-fashioned way but more and more of today's cooks, in an effort to save time and eliminate fats, prefer the quick-bake method used below.

Meatballs are basic to the cuisines of many of the ethnic groups that settled in our country. The sauces that follow are a quick way to adapt this basic recipe to Oriental-, Indian-, Italian- and Russian-style meals.

> Sauce of choice, see pages 10 to 12
> 1-1/2 pounds extra-lean ground beef or ground chuck
> 1/2 pound ground pork
> 3 tablespoons finely minced onion
> 1/2 cup soft bread crumbs
> 1/2 cup milk
> 2 eggs
> 1-1/2 teaspoons salt
> 1/2 teaspoon ground allspice (optional)
> 1/4 teaspoon ground white pepper (optional)

Prepare sauce of choice; set aside. In a large bowl, combine ground beef, ground pork, onion, bread crumbs, milk, eggs, salt, allspice and pepper, if used, until evenly blended. Preheat oven to 500F (260C). Shape meat mixture into balls the size of large marbles, using 1 tablespoon of mixture for each. Arrange meatballs on 1 or more large shallow baking pans. Bake 4 to 5 minutes or until lightly browned. Remove and add to prepared sauce including pan juices. Serve immediately or cool, then refrigerate until serving time. Reheat meatballs and sauce over low heat; keep warm in a chafing dish or over a candle warmer. Makes about 80 meatballs.

Note: For weddings, family gatherings or other large, group occasions, multiply the quantities and bake the meatballs ahead. Freeze them in a single layer on a tray. When frozen, pack them into plastic bags and return to the freezer. Meatballs may be easily thawed by adding them, still frozen, to a hot prepared sauce for serving.

Oriental-Style Sweet & Sour Meatballs

— • ◆ • —

Sweet and sour sauce means Oriental- or Polynesian-style to us. For a main dish, serve the meatballs over hot fluffy rice and offer extra soy sauce as a condiment. These meatballs make an excellent party appetizer, too. Keep hot in a chafing dish and have frilled picks handy.

> **Swedish Meatballs, page 9**
> **1 (16-ounce) can unsweetened pineapple chunks, packed in**
> **   natural juices**
> **1 (10-3/4-ounce) can undiluted chicken broth**
> **1/4 cup packed dark-brown sugar**
> **1/4 to 1/2 cup white-wine vinegar or to taste**
> **1 tablespoon soy sauce**
> **1 tablespoon tomato ketchup**
> **1/4 cup cornstarch**
> **1 cup sliced green onion**
> **3 green bell peppers, seeded, cut into 1-inch squares**

Prepare Swedish Meatballs; set aside. Drain juice from pineapple into a large heavy skillet. Add chicken broth, brown sugar, vinegar, soy sauce, ketchup and cornstarch. Whisk until blended. Stir over medium-high heat until mixture comes to a boil and thickens. Add onion and peppers. Cook 1 minute longer, stirring. Remove from heat. Add pineapple and baked meatballs with pan juices. Heat to serving temperature or cool and reheat later. Makes 6 to 8 main-dish servings, 20 appetizer servings.

Meatballs in Sour-Cream Stroganoff Sauce

— • ◆ • —

Sour cream in the sauce denotes to us a "Russian" flavor. Serve the meatballs in sauce over hot buttered noodles.

> **Swedish Meatballs, page 9**
> **1/4 cup butter**
> **1 small onion, minced**
> **1/4 cup all-purpose flour**
> **2-1/4 cups beef broth**
> **1/2 pint dairy sour cream (1 cup)**
> **1/2 teaspoon dill weed**
> **Salt and freshly ground black pepper to taste**

Prepare Swedish Meatballs; set aside. In a large heavy skillet, heat butter. Add onion. Cook over low heat, stirring, about 5 minutes or until onion is translucent but not browned. Blend in flour. Gradually stir in beef broth. Cook, stirring, until thickened. Stir in sour cream, dill weed, salt and pepper. Add baked meatballs with pan juices. Heat to serving temperature or cool and reheat later. Makes 6 to 8 main-dish servings, 20 appetizer servings.

Meatballs in Italian Tomato Sauce

Italians have probably had the greatest influence on American cuisine of all immigrant groups. Spaghetti and meatballs, pizza, lasagna, are a few of our popular family dishes that attest to this belief. Serve the basic meatballs over cooked pasta and offer additional grated Parmesan cheese for topping.

> **Swedish Meatballs, page 9, omitting allspice and adding 1**
> **teaspoon *each* dried leaf basil and oregano, and 1/2 teaspoon**
> ***each* garlic puree and freshly ground black pepper**
> **2 tablespoons olive oil**
> **1 medium-sized onion, chopped**
> **1 garlic clove, minced or mashed**
> **1 quart home-canned tomatoes or 1 (28-ounce) can Italian-style**
> **tomatoes**
> **1 teaspoon dried leaf basil**
> **1 teaspoon dried leaf oregano**
> **1 bay leaf**
> **1/4 cup red wine**
> **1 teaspoon sugar**
> **1 teaspoon salt**
> **1/4 teaspoon freshly ground black pepper**
> **1 cup (3 ounces) grated Parmesan cheese**

Prepare Swedish Meatballs making the changes listed above; set aside. In a large heavy skillet, heat olive oil. Add onion. Sauté 5 minutes over low heat. Add garlic and cook 1 minute. Add tomatoes with juice, basil, oregano and bay leaf. Simmer, uncovered, 20 minutes. Stir wine, sugar, salt and pepper into sauce. Add Parmesan cheese and baked meatballs with pan juices. Heat to serving temperature or cool and reheat later. Makes 6 to 8 main-dish servings, 20 appetizer servings.

Meatballs with Swedish Cream Gravy

This makes a perfect family dish.

> **Swedish Meatballs, page 9**
> **1/4 cup all-purpose flour**
> **2 cups half and half**
> **Salt and freshly ground black pepper to taste**

Prepare Swedish Meatballs; set aside. Strain juices from baking pan; set aside. In a large heavy skillet, stir flour over medium heat until browned. Slowly whisk in half and half, pan juices, salt and pepper; bring to a boil. Cook, stirring, until thickened and smooth. If gravy has lumps, pour through a strainer or turn into a blender and process until smooth. Add baked meatballs to sauce. Heat to serving temperature or cool and reheat later. Makes 6 to 8 main-dish servings.

Meatballs in Curry Sauce

—————————•◆•—————————

To enjoy meatballs curry-style, serve over hot fluffy rice and offer flaked or grated coconut, chopped almonds, chutney, sliced bananas and other favorite curry toppings.

Swedish Meatballs, page 9
1/4 cup butter
1 large onion, chopped
1 garlic clove, minced or mashed
2 tablespoons curry powder
3 tablespoons cornstarch
2 teaspoons sugar
1/2 teaspoon salt
Dash of red (cayenne) pepper
2 cups chicken broth
1/2 pint whipping cream (1 cup)

Prepare Swedish Meatballs; set aside. In a large heavy skillet, heat butter. Add onion and garlic. Sauté 5 minutes or until onion is translucent. Add curry powder and stir 1 minute. Stir in cornstarch, sugar, salt and red pepper over medium heat until bubbly. Gradually stir in chicken broth and cream. Cook, stirring, until thickened. Remove from heat and add baked meatballs with pan juices. Heat to serving temperature or cool and reheat later. Makes 6 to 8 main-dish servings, 20 appetizer servings.

Country-Style Meat Loaf

Meat loaves like this are an American invention. Europeans make pâtés and various loaves with highly seasoned ground meats. When ground meats became a mainstay in the American kitchen in the 20th century, we developed meat loaves. Meat loaves that are dry are so because they have been overcooked, or because they have too much oatmeal, rice, corn flakes or cereals for binders. This one is very juicy. Delicious served hot, it is also excellent served cold or used as a filling for sandwiches.

> 2 pounds extra-lean ground beef
> 1 medium-sized onion, sliced crosswise into rings
> 2 eggs, unbeaten
> 1-1/2 teaspoons mustard powder
> 1 teaspoon chili powder
> 1 pint home-canned tomatoes or 1 (16-ounce) can whole, diced,
>   sliced or wedged tomatoes
> 2 bread slices, broken into pieces
> 1-1/2 teaspoons salt
> 1/4 teaspoon freshly ground black pepper
> 4 bacon slices

Preheat oven to 350F (175C). In the bowl of a heavy-duty mixer, combine beef, onion, eggs, mustard powder, chili powder, tomatoes with juice, bread, salt and pepper. Mix until ingredients are evenly blended. Or, mix thoroughly with your hands in a large bowl. Pack mixture into a 9″ x 5″ loaf pan. Place bacon slices on top of meat mixture. Bake 1-1/2 hours. Makes 8 to 10 servings.

Old-Time Meat Loaf with Salt Pork

The original term "meat packer" meant somebody who packed meat in barrels with salt. Salt pork was the standard meat of Americans heading Westward.

> 2 pounds lean ground beef
> 1/4 pound salt pork, ground
> 3/4 cup fine dry bread crumbs
> 1 cup hot milk
> 1 egg
> 1 teaspoon crumbled, dried, sage leaves
> 1/4 teaspoon celery salt
> 1/4 teaspoon freshly ground black pepper
> Relish

Preheat oven to 350F (175C). In a large bowl, blend beef with salt pork; push to side of bowl. On the other side of bowl, mix 1/2 cup bread crumbs with hot milk. Blend meat, crumb mixture, egg, sage, celery salt and pepper. Press into a 9″ x 5″ loaf pan. Top with remaining bread crumbs. Bake 1 hour. Serve hot with relish of choice. Makes 8 servings.

Serbian Sarmas or Cabbage Rolls

— ◆ —

Almost every European ethnic group claims stuffed cabbage rolls. The Slavs, Slovenians, Czechs and other Eastern Europeans also traditionally made sauerkraut from their bumper crop of cabbage every fall. My friend, a lady of Czech background, recalls that her farm home always had the smell of sauerkraut which was served all winter long with many kinds of stewed meats, pork roasts, meatballs, meat loaves and cabbage rolls.

> 1 large head cabbage
> 1/4 pound ground pork
> 3/4 pound ground beef
> 1/2 cup long-grain rice, cooked 10 minutes, rinsed, drained
> 1 small onion, chopped
> 2 garlic cloves, mashed (optional)
> 1 egg
> 3/4 teaspoon salt
> 1/4 teaspoon freshly ground black pepper
> 1 (2-pound) package refrigerated sauerkraut or 1 (32-ounce) can
> 1 (8-ounce) can tomato sauce
> 2 tablespoons brown sugar
> 1 cup beef broth

Carefully remove large outer leaves from cabbage; you will need 12 leaves. Wash leaves. Drop into a large pot of boiling water for 5 minutes or until leaves are just flexible. Remove and drain. Preheat oven to 350F (175C). In a large bowl, combine ground pork, ground beef, rice, onion, garlic, if desired, egg, salt and pepper. Divide meat mixture evenly to make 12 balls. Place 1 ball of meat on each cabbage leaf; wrap leaves tightly to enclose meat. Rinse and drain sauerkraut. Spread in the bottom of a large shallow baking pan. Place filled cabbage leaves on top of sauerkraut. In a small saucepan, combine tomato sauce, brown sugar and beef broth. Stir and bring to a boil. Pour over rolls. Bake, uncovered, 1 hour. Add more liquid if necessary during cooking. Makes 12 cabbage rolls.

Variation
German-Style Cabbage Rolls: Omit sauerkraut and beef broth. Add 1/4 cup cider vinegar and 1 (12-ounce) bottle or can of beer to tomato-sauce mixture. Bake as above. Serve with buttered cooked noodles.

Chili con Carne

—— ·♦· ——

Chili con carne is said to have been invented by Mexican residents of Texas. J.C. Clopper, a reporter visiting San Antonio in 1828, described the dish this way: "When they have to pay for their meat in the market, a very little is made to suffice a family; it is generally cut into a kind of hash with nearly as many peppers as there are pieces of meat. This is all stewed together."

Edward King, a Northerner writing in 1874, complained that the "fiery pepper biteth like a serpent." But O'Henry liked it. He said it was a "compound full of singular savor and a fiery zest."

> 2 pounds extra-lean ground beef
> 1 large onion, chopped
> 2 garlic cloves, minced or pressed
> 1 quart skinned fresh tomatoes or home-canned tomatoes, or
>   2 (16-ounce) cans tomatoes
> 1 (8-ounce) can tomato sauce
> 4 cups beef broth
> 2 to 3 tablespoons chili powder
> 1 tablespoon ground cumin
> Salt to taste
> 1/2 teaspoon dried leaf oregano
> Dash of hot-pepper sauce
> 2 cups pinto beans, cooked*, or 2 (16-ounce) cans pinto or red
>   kidney beans, drained

In a heavy Dutch oven, slowly brown beef with onion and garlic until meat is cooked through. Add tomatoes with juice, tomato sauce, beef broth, chili powder, cumin, salt, oregano and hot-pepper sauce. Simmer beef mixture, covered, 1-1/2 to 2 hours. Add cooked or canned beans and simmer 30 minutes longer. Makes 8 servings.

*To cook pinto beans: Follow package directions. Or, wash and pick over beans; place in a large saucepan. Cover with water and soak overnight. Drain. Cover with water again. Simmer, covered, 2 to 3 hours or until beans are tender.
For the "quick-soak" method: Wash and pick over beans; place in a large saucepan. Cover with water and bring to a boil. Remove from heat. Cover and let stand 1 hour. Return to a simmer and cook, covered, 3 to 4 hours or until beans are tender.

New Mexico Tamale Pie

· ◆ ·

Many so-called Mexican dishes are not so much Spanish as they are Indian. This dish is credited to the Aztecs who served it to Cortes when he arrived in Mexico City. Traditional tamales are made with corn husks that have been soaked in water, spread with cornmeal mush made from *masa*, and sometimes topped with chili con carne. The husks are folded up to enclose the filling, tied with another strip of husk, then steamed until heated through. Tamale pie has basically the same ingredients without the corn husks and is baked in a casserole lined with cornmeal masa. It makes a great meal accompanied by a garlicky green salad and followed with a platter of fresh melons for dessert.

2-1/2 cups boiling water
1 cup yellow cornmeal
2 teaspoons salt
2 tablespoons butter
1/2 cup whole ripe olives
1/2 cup raisins
1 cup (4 ounces) shredded Jack or Cheddar cheese

Filling:
2 tablespoons vegetable oil
1/2 cup diced white onion
1 garlic clove, minced or pressed
1 pound lean ground beef
1/2 cup diced celery
1/4 cup diced green bell pepper
1 cup whole-kernel corn, fresh from the cob, frozen or drained,
   canned
1-1/2 cups chopped fresh tomatoes
1 cup sliced ripe olives
1 tablespoon chili powder
2 teaspoons salt
1/4 teaspoon ground allspice
1/4 teaspoon freshly ground black pepper

Boil water in a medium-sized saucepan. Stir in cornmeal and salt. Cook until thickened, stirring constantly. Add butter. Cook, stirring, 20 minutes over low heat. Grease a 2-quart casserole. Spread cooked cornmeal over bottom and sides of casserole. Set aside while you prepare filling. Preheat oven to 350F (175C). Pour filling into lined casserole. Bake 45 minutes. Before serving, sprinkle top with whole ripe olives, raisins and shredded cheese. Return to oven just long enough to melt cheese. Makes 6 to 8 servings. **To prepare filling:** In a heavy skillet, heat oil. Add onion and garlic. Sauté over low heat 5 minutes. Increase heat to high and add beef. Brown meat, stirring constantly. Add celery, green pepper, corn, tomatoes, sliced olives and seasonings. Simmer over low heat 10 minutes.

Cowboy Steak

•◆•

The image of cowboys holding a steak on a stick over an open fire was my first impression of this recipe. Careful reading, however, indicates that the cowboy must have had a "missus" back at camp marinating this steak while her man was out rounding up the "doggies" (calves).

This makes a great, economical, company dish! Look for a thick, boneless, first cut of the chuck at the meat counter. It is usually the least expensive of the chuck roasts. The thicker 2-inch cut will be juicier and more tender if you use a smoke-cooker.

> 1 (1-1/2- to 2-inch-thick) boneless chuck roast, preferably the
>   first cut (5 to 5-1/2 pounds)
> 2 garlic cloves, minced
> 2 tablespoons vegetable oil
> 1 tablespoon soy sauce
> 1/2 teaspoon dried leaf rosemary
> 1/4 teaspoon mustard powder
> 1/3 cup red-wine vinegar
> 2 teaspoons freshly ground black pepper

Trim excess fat from roast. Place roast in a shallow baking dish or in a large, heavy-duty, plastic bag. Combine remaining ingredients and spread over both sides of meat. Cover and refrigerate 24 hours, turning 2 or 3 times. The next day, preheat broiler or charcoal. Broil meat about 5 inches from heat about 20 minutes on 1 side and 15 minutes on the other. Or, cook in a charcoal-fired smoke-cooker 5 to 6 hours or until meat registers 140F (60C) for rare or 150F (65C) for medium rare. The long slow cooking combined with the initial marinating makes the meat very tender. To serve, cut across grain on diagonal. Makes about 1 serving per 1/3 pound of uncooked meat.

Note: Use an instant reading thermometer to check the temperature of the meat quickly. This is a type of thermometer designed for use with microwaved foods, also one that chef's carry around with them to check the temperature of sauces. The very slim stem on the thermometer allows an almost instant temperature reading.

Mesquite Barbecued Steaks

Mesquite, a tree or shrub that is a member of the pea family, grows in the dry areas of the Southwestern United States. Because of its ability to withstand extreme heat and drought, it thrives in desert regions with roots that may go down 70 feet into the earth. It produces pods filled with a sweet pulp which are edible and used as animal food in regions where green foliage is rare. Although the use of the shrub is rather new to today's barbecue enthusiasts, it has been used as an aromatic source of heat for barbecuing since the days of the pioneers in the West. Steaks cooked over mesquite wood are excellent served with large Ranch-Style Biscuits, page 140.

Chicken-Fried Steak

—◆—

In the West where steak was abundant and chickens were scarce, this was an economical and popular way to prepare round steak or minute steak. This is sometimes called *Texas-fried steak*. The meat is rolled in flour or crumbs, fried and eaten like chicken.

> **1 cup dry bread crumbs**
> **1/2 teaspoon salt**
> **1/4 teaspoon freshly ground black pepper**
> **8 thin slices round steak or minute steak (1 pound)**
> **1 large egg, beaten**
> **1/4 cup vegetable oil**
> **2 tablespoons all-purpose flour**
> **1 cup water or milk**
> **Additional salt and freshly ground pepper (optional)**

On a plate, mix bread crumbs with 1/2 teaspoon salt and 1/4 teaspoon pepper. Dip beef into beaten egg, then into bread crumbs. In a heavy skillet, heat oil. Add meat. Brown over low heat 10 to 15 minutes on each side. Place on a warm platter; keep hot. To make gravy, add flour to pan drippings. Stir over medium heat until light brown. With a whisk, stir in water or milk until it thickens into gravy. Add more liquid if too thick. If desired, add salt and pepper to taste. Return steaks to pan. Simmer until ready to serve. Makes 4 servings.

Round Steak & Onions

—◆—

This is also known as *Swiss steak* and often has cheese sprinkled on top before serving.

> **1 to 1-1/2 pounds round steak**
> **1/2 teaspoon salt**
> **1/4 teaspoon freshly ground black pepper**
> **1/2 teaspoon dried leaf marjoram**
> **1/4 cup all-purpose flour**
> **1/4 cup butter**
> **2 medium-sized onions, thinly sliced**
> **1/2 cup beef broth**
> **1/2 cup dairy sour cream**

Cut steak into 4 pieces. On a plate, mix salt, pepper, marjoram and flour. Dredge steak in flour mixture. With the side of a plate, pound flour mixture into steaks, adding more of mixture until steaks are about doubled in diameter and about 1/4 inch thick. In a heavy skillet, heat butter over medium heat. Add onions. Sauté 10 minutes or until golden. Lift out onions; set aside. Add steak to hot fat; brown over medium-high heat. Add beef broth and sautéed onions. Cover and simmer over very low heat 1 hour or until steaks are fork-tender. Remove steaks onto a warm platter. Stir sour cream into pan drippings, whisking until smooth. Pour over steaks and serve. Makes 4 servings.

Pan-Fried Porterhouse with Mushrooms

When Mark Twain toured Europe in 1878, he complained bitterly about the food. One of the favorites marked on his list of foods to be ready and hot when he arrived at home was a porterhouse steak, pan-fried, with mushrooms.

> **1/2 cup butter**
> **1 pound fresh mushrooms, sliced**
> **1 teaspoon dried leaf tarragon**
> **3/4 cup whipping cream**
> **1 (1-1/2-inch-thick) porterhouse steak (about 2 pounds)**
> **1 tablespoon butter**
> **Salt and freshly ground black pepper to taste**

In a skillet or frying pan, heat 1/2 cup butter. Add mushrooms. Sauté over medium heat 5 minutes. Add tarragon and cream. Simmer over low heat until sauce has thickened slightly. Score fat on steak so it will not curl during cooking. Place 1 tablespoon butter and steak in another heavy skillet. Cook steak over high heat 5 minutes on each side for rare meat. Or, cook longer according to your taste. Sprinkle with salt and pepper. Serve with creamed mushrooms. Makes 2 to 3 servings.

New England Boiled Dinner

• ◆ •

For a boiled dinner, a genuine Yankee cook uses brisket, the classic cut for making corned beef. The meat is covered with cold water and simmered gently until almost tender, then the vegetables are added. Strangers to New England are alarmed at the absence of the red color which is characteristic of corned beef. But this beef is not cured with saltpeter which would give that red color. The beets are usually boiled separately as they tend to dye everything red. The traditional dish for the day following a boiled dinner is one of Red Flannel Hash which utilizes the leftovers from this meal.

> **1 (3- to 4-pound) lean beef brisket or corned beef**
> **8 medium-sized onions, peeled**
> **1 small head cabbage, cut into wedges**
> **8 large carrots, cut into chunks**
> **2 white turnips, cut into 1/2-inch slices**
> **8 medium-sized potatoes, quartered**
> **8 whole beets**
> **Salt and freshly ground black pepper to taste**
> **Melted butter (optional)**
> **Freshly grated horseradish (optional)**

Place meat in a deep heavy pot. Add water to cover. Simmer 3 to 4 hours or until meat is fork-tender. Add whole onions, cabbage, carrots, turnips and potatoes. Simmer 20 to 30 minutes longer or until vegetables are tender. Meanwhile, place beets in a separate pot. Add water to cover. Simmer until tender. Peel cooked beets. To serve, slice beef and arrange vegetables around it on a large platter. In the classic arrangement, carrots and turnips are at opposite ends. Cabbage wedges and beets are on opposite sides of platter from potatoes and onions. Season with salt and pepper. Pour melted butter over vegetables, if desired. Serve with Northern Johnnycake or Corn Bread, page 142, Beaten Biscuits, page 139, or white rolls. Freshly grated horseradish can be passed at the table. Apple Pie, page 188, completes the menu. Makes 4 servings with enough leftovers for Red Flannel Hash, opposite.

Red Flannel Hash

---•◆•---

This hash is usually prepared on the day after a New England Boiled Dinner which included cooked beets. It is the beets that give it the "red flannel" name.

    3 medium-sized beets, cooked
    1 large potato, cooked
    1 pound ground cooked meat
    Salt and freshly ground black pepper to taste
    1/2 cup butter
    1 medium-sized onion, chopped
    1 tablespoon whipping cream

Grease a 2-quart baking dish. Chop beets and potato using a knife, or chop in a food processor fitted with the steel blade until coarse but not fine. Turn into a medium-sized bowl. Mix in ground meat, salt and pepper. In a large skillet, heat half of butter. Add onion. Cook over medium heat 5 minutes or until onion is translucent. Stir in meat mixture. Cook over low heat 10 minutes, stirring occasionally. Preheat broiler. Lift mixture into greased baking dish. Melt remaining butter and combine with cream. Spoon over hash. Broil 3 inches from heat 5 minutes or until hash has a rich brown crust. May be served with poached eggs on top. Makes 4 servings.

Shepherd's Pie

---•◆•---

The Farmer magazine first published a recipe for this classic Shepherd's Pie in January, 1912 as a suggestion for a way to serve cold leftover roast or steak. Its wonderfully simple name and unpretentious character prompted a young family we know to make this their Christmas Eve meal every year because it provides a plain yet tasty contrast to the rich food served on Christmas Day.

    1-1/2 cups ground cooked meat
    1 cup hot beef broth or leftover beef gravy
    1 small onion, sliced
    Salt and freshly ground black pepper to taste
    2 cups mashed potatoes
    1/4 cup half and half or milk
    1 to 2 tablespoons butter, softened

Preheat oven to 350F (175C). In a medium-sized bowl, combine meat with broth or gravy and onion. Add salt and pepper. Turn into a heavy skillet and heat to simmering. Pour into a baking dish. Whip potatoes with half and half or milk, butter, salt and pepper. Beat until light. Spread whipped potato mixture over meat mixture to cover completely. Bake 30 to 40 minutes or until lightly browned. Makes 4 servings.

Iron Miners' Pasties

— ◆ —

Iron miners in Northern Minnesota and in the copper mines of the Upper Peninsula of Michigan carried pasties in their lunchpails everyday to the depths of the mines. The pasties were often baked fresh in the morning and wrapped so they would stay hot until lunchtime. The most commonly known pasties are simply filled with beef, potatoes, carrots and onions. In order to have a hot "dessert," some miners' wives baked an apple filling into one end of the pasty. This makes an excellent picnic pie.

Boiling-Water Pastry:
1 cup lard or shortening
1-1/4 cups boiling water
1 teaspoon salt
4-1/2 to 5 cups all-purpose flour

Beef-Vegetable Filling:
4 medium-sized potatoes, cut into 1/2-inch dice
1 cup diced carrots (1/2-inch dice)
1 large onion, chopped
1 teaspoon salt
1/2 teaspoon freshly ground black pepper
1 pound top round of beef, cut into 1/2-inch pieces

Apple Filling:
4 medium-sized apples, pared, cored, sliced into
** 12 wedges each**
2 tablespoons sugar
2 teaspoons all-purpose flour
1/2 teaspoon ground cinnamon
1/8 teaspoon salt

To prepare Boiling-Water Pastry: In a large bowl, mix lard or shortening with boiling water and salt; stir until fat is melted. Add enough flour to make a stiff dough. Cover and refrigerate 1 hour or more. Divide into 8 parts. On a lightly floured board, roll out each part to make an oval, 11 inches long and 8 inches across. Preheat oven to 350F (175C). Line 2 baking sheets with parchment paper or grease baking sheets.
To prepare Beef-Vegetable Filling: In a medium-sized bowl, combine ingredients.
To prepare Apple Filling: In another medium-sized bowl, combine ingredients.
To fill and bake: Put 1 cup meat mixture on center of each pastry oval, leaving enough space on 1 side for the length of the apple slices, and 2 to 2-1/2 inches of margin along both sides of filling. Arrange 6 apple slices in a little pile on empty side of pastry oval, next to meat filling. Gently lift pastry edge up around meat and apple fillings. Pinch seam firmly lengthwise across top of pastry to make a seam about 1/2 inch wide and standing upright. Pinch with 2 fingers and thumb to make a pretty rope-like design. Repeat for each pasty. Place a wooden pick on end of pasty to mark apple end of filling. Arrange pasties on prepared baking sheets. Bake 1 hour or until golden. Serve hot, cooled to room temperature, or refrigerate, or freeze. Heat in a 300F (150C) oven before serving. Pasties are usually served with a pat of butter on top. Makes 8 pasties.

Sauerbraten

· ◆ ·

The Pennsylvania Dutch and their ancestors have traditionally been meat eaters. The early settlers, however, had to settle for rabbit, wild fowl and venison until their herds were established. It took many years before they could afford to butcher a steer because beef was a primary source of income and was sold in the market place rather than kept for family use. Because of a lack of feed, swine were allowed to forage in the woods for the first years and the resulting meat was tough and required long cooking to tenderize it. But the Dutch hausfrau was a good cook and knew how to tenderize coarse meat with spiced vinegar mixtures, as in this "sour roast."

> **4 pounds boneless, rolled beef chuck or round**
> **Salt and pepper**
> **3 cups white or cider vinegar**
> **3 cups water**
> **4 large onions, sliced**
> **1 bay leaf**
> **1 teaspoon whole black peppercorns**
> **2 tablespoons sugar**
> **10 whole cloves**
> **All-purpose flour**
> **2 tablespoons lard or vegetable oil**
> **Crumbera Knepp, page 24**
> **3 tablespoons all-purpose flour**
> **1/4 teaspoon ground ginger**
> **1/4 teaspoon ground allspice**
> **1/2 cup raisins**

Rub beef with salt and pepper. Place in a large, stainless, glass or plastic bowl (not aluminum). In a large saucepan, combine vinegar, water, onions, bay leaf, peppercorns, sugar and cloves. Heat just to simmering; do not boil. Pour vinegar mixture over beef to partially cover. Cool, then cover and refrigerate 4 to 6 days, turning meat each day. Remove meat from marinade, reserving marinade. Wipe meat dry. Rub meat with flour. Heat lard or oil in a heavy Dutch oven. Brown meat on all sides in hot fat. Pour vinegar mixture over beef. Taste and dilute with water if it seems too sour. Reduce heat. Simmer, covered, 2 to 3 hours or until meat is tender and vinegar mixture cooked down. Prepare potato balls for Crumbera Knepp. Remove beef and keep warm. Strain liquid and return to Dutch oven. In a cup, mix 3 tablespoons flour with a small amount of water to make a paste; whisk into liquid in Dutch oven. Bring to a boil and cook, whisking, until thickened. Add ginger, allspice and raisins. Cook potato balls for Crumbera Knepp. Moisten roast with gravy and serve remainder in a gravy boat. Serve meat with hot dumplings. Makes 8 servings.

Crumbera Knepp

◆

These potato dumplings are boiled like noodles and served hot with Sauerbraten, page 23.

> 4 large potatoes, unpared
> 1/2 cup bread crumbs
> 1 egg
> 2 tablespoons milk
> 1/2 teaspoon salt
> 1 tablespoon all-purpose flour

Place unpared potatoes in a medium-sized saucepan. Add water to cover. Simmer about 25 minutes or until cooked. Let potatoes cool in their skins. Peel and put through a ricer. In a large bowl, mix bread crumbs, egg and milk; stir in riced potatoes and salt. If batter is too stiff and crumbly, add another egg. Mold into balls the size of walnuts. Dust with flour. Bring a large pot of water to a boil. Add 1 tablespoon salt for each quart of water. Drop potato balls into boiling water. Cover and boil gently 10 minutes. Serve immediately. Makes 8 servings.

Liver with Bacon in Sour-Cream Gravy

◆

We have available three kinds of liver: beef liver from mature animals; baby beef liver from animals up to 12 months old; and calves' liver from animals between one and three months in age. Any kind of liver can be used here, but I prefer calves' liver.

> 8 bacon slices
> 1 large onion, sliced
> 1 pound calves' liver, thinly sliced
> 1 egg
> 1/2 cup milk
> 1/2 cup all-purpose flour
> 3/4 teaspoon salt
> 1/4 teaspoon freshly ground black pepper
> 1/2 pint dairy sour cream (1 cup)

In a large heavy skillet, cook bacon over medium to low heat until crisp. Remove bacon onto a warm serving platter. Add onion to skillet. Cook over low heat 10 minutes or until soft but not browned. Remove to platter with bacon. Drain liver and pat dry with paper towels. In a shallow dish such as a pie pan, beat egg and milk together until blended. Mix flour, salt and pepper in another shallow dish. Dip liver pieces first in egg mixture, then into flour mixture. Increase heat to medium-high. Add liver pieces. Brown quickly on both sides, about 5 minutes. Liver cooks quickly and is best when not overdone and dry. Remove meat to platter with onions and bacon. Add sour cream to skillet; stir to scrape up brownings. Pour sauce over liver and serve immediately. Makes 4 servings.

✦ PORK, LAMB & GAME ✦

Although wild pigs were found in Mexico by Cortes in the late 1400s, swine have probably been domesticated since the Stone Age. It is said that Hernando de Soto brought a herd of 13 pigs to Florida in the mid-1500s.

Pork was the most important source of meat in early America. Colonists turned their swine into the woods for foraging and rounded them up in the fall for butchering. The animals developed strong muscles making the meat stringy and tough. Pork whether fresh or cured, required long, slow, moist cooking to make it tender enough to be palatable.

Butchering day on the early American farm turned it into a factory from dawn to dark. Hams and bacon were put to cure and later smoked. They produced roasts, steaks and chops which were brined for preservation. Meat scraps and offal were turned into liverwurst, headcheese, sausages, bologna and other preserved meats. The Pennsylvania Dutch also made scrapple with meat scraps and cornmeal.

Old cookbooks go into detail about how to cut up a carcass of pork, and how to salt, cure and smoke the pieces. Everything was used including the blood for sausages, puddings and pancakes and the intestines for sausage casings. The ears and snouts are high in gelatin and are valuable even today for making headcheese and cold cuts. The fatty "sides" were cured and salted or smoked into bacon. The original term "packer" came to mean somebody who packed pork into barrels of salt. Salt pork was the standard food of the Westward-bound pioneers. Even the skin was tanned into a fine leather and the tallow made into soap.

Lamb and mutton have never gained the same acceptance as pork and beef. One reason may be that American lamb is butchered at a relatively late age and the flavor is quite strong. An animal less than a year old is classified as "lamb," then it becomes "mutton."

While the domesticated animals were being raised, people had to make do with rabbit, venison and other game. *The Buckeye Cookbook*, published in 1883, printed 27 pages of game

Continued on page 26.

recipes to include all edible wild animals and fowl. The book gives complete directions for singeing, drawing and dressing many birds including woodcock, quail, reed birds, prairie chickens, snipe, wild ducks, teal, pheasants, grouse, geese and "all small birds." In addition, it states that, "Squirrels should be carefully skinned and laid in salt water a short time before cooking, and if old, parboil."

You won't find any squirrel dishes among the recipes that follow but I did include some favorites using rabbit and venison.

Baked Spiced Ham

The smokehouse of the Old South was a structure about 10 feet square. After preliminary curing with dry salt and seasonings, or after soaking in a brine of salt mixed with saltpeter, sugar and other ingredients, the meat was sacked and hung to smoke in the smokehouse. Hickory, added for fragrance and flavor, was used whenever possible. Sometimes corncobs were added. The hams were smoked for several days until they turned a mahogany brown. After smoking, the hams were aged for at least 16 to 18 months. Virginia ham is recognized as one of America's great achievements. Today, three kinds of hams are well-known. These are "country," the original work of art, and two that are 19th century developments, "Smithfield," and "Western" or "packinghouse" ham.

This original recipe is from *The Williamsburg Art of Cookery*, and is said to have been the recipe used by Jefferson's family at Monticello. My recipe that follows is updated.

"Select a nicely cured Ham. Soak overnight in cold water. Wipe off and put in enough Water to cover. Simmer for three Hours. Let cool in the water it was cooked in. Take out and trim. Put into Baking pan. Stick with Cloves and cover with brown Sugar. Bake in a moderate Oven for two Hours. Baste with White Wine. Serve with a savory Salad."

> 1 whole (10- to 12-pound) cured, smoked, (uncooked) ham
> 1/4 cup whole cloves
> 1 cup packed dark-brown sugar
> 2 cups dry white wine
> Additional white wine
> 1 tablespoon Dijon-style mustard
> Parsley sprigs
> Fried apple slices

Place ham in a large pot; add cold water to cover. Refrigerate overnight. Drain. Add fresh water to cover. Bring to a boil over high heat. Reduce heat; skim off any fat. Cover and simmer 3 hours. Add more water to keep meat covered, if necessary. Remove from heat and cool in cooking liquid. Preheat oven to 325F (165C). Remove ham from liquid. Trim excess fat. Place ham on a rack in a baking pan. Stick whole cloves into ham forming a grid or diamond pattern. Pat on a thin layer of brown sugar. Bake 2 hours. Baste with 2 cups white wine while baking. Place on a warm platter. Skim fat from baking pan. Deglaze pan by scraping up brownings with additional white wine. Bring to a boil and cook down until juices make a thick glaze. Whisk in mustard. Brush ham with glaze until shiny. Garnish with parsley and fried apples. Makes 3 to 4 servings per pound.

Note: To make fried apples, slice whole apples crosswise; do not remove skin or core. Fry in a small amount of butter until browned on both sides but not cooked through.

Country Ham with Red-Eye Gravy

—————————————— ◆ ——————————————

Red-eye gravy is another recipe that can start an argument! There are only three ingredients in the recipe but the disagreement storms over whether the pan juices are thinned with water or coffee! In some places, it is served with Hush Puppies, page 144, in others fried biscuits. In either case, the bread is fried.

6 slices (1/4-inch-thick) well-smoked country ham
1/4 cup packed brown sugar
1/2 cup double-strength black coffee or water

Trim fat off ham. Sauté fat in a heavy skillet until enough fat is rendered to coat bottom of skillet. Add ham. Cook, turning several times until heated through. Remove ham and keep warm. Stir brown sugar into drippings. Cook over low heat, stirring constantly, until sugar melts. Add coffee or water. Stir 5 minutes or until mixture is a rich red-brown color. Spoon gravy onto a warm serving platter and top with ham slices. Makes 6 servings.

Maryland-Style Stuffed Baked Ham

—— ◆ ——

This is an attractive way to present the holiday ham. The green of the spinach contrasts with the red of the ham making a handsomely appropriate dish for the Christmas table.

1 fully cooked ham (about 10 pounds)
1 (10-ounce) package frozen chopped kale or collard greens
1 cup finely chopped fresh spinach
1 large onion, chopped
3/4 cup chopped watercress
1/2 cup finely chopped celery tops
1/2 teaspoon salt
1/4 teaspoon freshly ground black pepper
1/2 cup honey
2 tablespoons vinegar
2 teaspoons mustard powder
Whole fresh spinach leaves

Preheat oven to 325F (165C). Trim rind from ham. With a small paring knife, make X-shaped cuts 2 inches deep and 1 inch apart, spacing cuts all over ham. Cook kale or collard greens according to package directions. Cool. Squeeze out all excess water. In a large bowl, combine greens, chopped spinach, onion, watercress, celery tops, salt and pepper. Press greens mixture into ham cuts, packing in well. Place ham, fat-side up, in a large shallow baking pan. Bake 2 hours. In a small bowl, blend honey, vinegar and mustard powder. Brush over ham. Continue baking and brushing with remaining honey mixture 30 minutes or until top of ham is richly glazed. To garnish, press fresh spinach leaves into cuts containing cooked greens. Let stand 20 minutes before carving. Makes about 12 servings.

Philadelphia Scrapple

─────────────────◆─────────────────

The Pennsylvania Dutch call this *Ponhaws*. It was originally a thrifty way to use scraps of pork after hogs had been butchered. Today, it can be an economical way to use the leftovers from a pork roast. Even though the recipe calls for fresh pork shoulder, you might roast a piece of pork shoulder 2 pounds larger than you plan to serve at a meal and use the remaining meat for making scrapple. The pork is mixed with cooked cornmeal, chilled in a loaf pan, then sliced and fried as desired.

> **2 pounds fresh pork shoulder**
> **1-1/2 quarts water**
> **1 teaspoon salt**
> **1/2 teaspoon freshly ground black pepper**
> **2 cups cornmeal**
> **1 teaspoon dried leaf summer savory**
> **1/2 teaspoon dried leaf thyme**
> **Additional salt and freshly ground black pepper (optional)**

Place pork in a Dutch oven. Add water, salt and pepper. Bring to a boil. Reduce heat and simmer 45 minutes to 1 hour or until meat comes away from bone easily. Remove meat. Strain broth; there should be about 4 cups broth. Shred meat. Return to Dutch oven with broth. Place over medium heat and slowly stir in cornmeal, keeping mixture smooth. Add savory, thyme and more salt and pepper to taste, if necessary. Simmer 15 minutes or until cornmeal is cooked. Press mixture into 2 (9″ x 5″) loaf pans. Refrigerate. To serve, cut into slices and fry in butter. Makes about 32 slices.

Garlicky Country-Style Pork Roast

─────────────────◆─────────────────

"Modern" pork is much leaner than it used to be and we have a wide range of prices you can pay for high-quality meat. Pork butt, which is actually a shoulder cut, is the least-expensive yet one of the tastiest cuts. The loin roasts, whether bone-in or bone-out are meatier with larger muscle structure, making carving nice slices easier. I prefer the rolled pork loin for this all-time favorite country-style pork roast, but the days before payday, I might settle for a butt cut on a supermarket special!

> **1 (5- to 8-pound) rolled pork loin or butt roast**
> **3 garlic cloves, minced**
> **2 teaspoons freshly ground black pepper**
> **2 teaspoons dried leaf rosemary**
> **1 teaspoon coarse kosher-style salt**
> **2 tablespoons vegetable oil or olive oil**

Place roast on a rack over a roasting pan. Combine garlic, pepper, rosemary, salt and oil. Rub evenly all over roast. Insert a meat thermometer into thickest part of meat. Place in oven and set at 350F (175C). Roast 1 to 2 hours or until thermometer registers 160F (70C) to 165F (75C). Let stand 20 minutes before carving. Makes 3 servings per pound.

Baked Stuffed Pork Chops

———————————— ◆ ————————————

Today's pork is leaner and cooks quickly. It's best cooked using slow, even, moist cooking to bring out flavor and make it juicy.

4 (1-1/2-inch-thick) pork loin chops
1/4 cup butter
2 garlic cloves, minced
1 medium-sized onion, chopped
1/2 cup chopped celery
1/2 cup chopped green bell pepper
2 cups soft bread crumbs
About 1 cup beef or chicken broth
Salt and freshly ground black pepper to taste
1/4 cup all-purpose flour
Chopped fresh parsley

Preheat oven to 325F (165C). With a sharp pointed knife, cut a slit in each pork chop for stuffing. In a large, heavy, ovenproof skillet or stove-top casserole, heat 2 tablespoons butter. Add garlic, onion, celery and green pepper. Sauté over low heat about 10 minutes or until soft. Mix with bread crumbs. Add about 1/2 cup broth to moisten so mixture holds together. Add salt and black pepper. Stuff each pork chop with one-quarter of mixture. Close each chop with a wooden pick. Sprinkle with salt, pepper and flour. Melt remaining butter in skillet. Add stuffed chops. Brown quickly on both sides. Add 1/2 cup broth. Cover with lid or foil. Bake 30 to 40 minutes or until chops are cooked through. Garnish with chopped parsley. Makes 4 servings.

Pork Chops with Lima Beans

— • ♦ • —

Except for game, pork is America's most traditional meat. The earliest settlers brought pigs with them, and they were let loose to fatten in the woods. Pork farmers have come a long way in breeding leaner, higher protein pork. For that reason, it is important not to overcook it or the meat will be dry.

4 large pork chops
1/4 cup all-purpose flour
1/2 teaspoon *each* dried sage, salt and pepper
1/4 cup butter or vegetable shortening
1 (10-ounce) package frozen lima beans, partially thawed
1 large onion, sliced into rings
1 cup apple cider or apple juice
1/2 cup whipping cream
2 chopped green onions

Preheat oven to 350F (175C). Wipe pork chops; set aside. In a small bowl, combine flour, sage, salt and pepper. Dredge pork chops in flour mixture. In a large heavy skillet, heat butter or shortening. Add pork chops. Brown over medium heat on both sides. Put chops into a shallow baking dish. Top with lima beans and onions. Pour cider or juice into skillet in which chops were browned; scrape up drippings. Pour over chops in baking dish. Bake 45 minutes; pour cream over. Bake 15 minutes longer. Top with chopped green onions. Serve hot. Makes 4 servings.

Farmhouse Breakfast Sausage

·◆·

When farmers did their own butchering, there were lots of scraps left over and these were made into sausages. Sausages are basic to many cuisines, but especially German, Swiss, Dutch, French and Scandinavian. The taste of the sausages reflected the flavorings favored by each ethnic group. Today, about the only sausage people might make at home is made from game, or just for the fun of it. For the uninitiated, the first thought would be that sausage should be made of very lean meat; not true. For juiciness, the meat should be at least 30% fat. If you purchase a pork butt roast, the fat percentage is about right. Grind it yourself, or ask the butcher to do it for you. Then have some fun seasoning and flavoring your own sausages.

2 pounds fresh pork butt, coarsely ground
1-1/2 teaspoons dried leaf thyme
1 teaspoon crumbled, dried, sage leaves
1 teaspoon salt
3/4 teaspoon freshly ground black pepper
1/4 teaspoon red (cayenne) pepper
About 2 ounces salted sausage casings (optional)

In a large bowl, blend pork, thyme, sage, salt, black pepper and red pepper. Refrigerate overnight for flavors to blend. Shape into patties. Cook in a heavy skillet over medium heat until cooked through, turning once.

For link sausages, purchase salted sausage casings from the meat market. Soak in cold water to remove salt, then slip end of casing over faucet in kitchen sink. Run cold water through to flush out inside of casings. This is more easily done if casings are cut into 20- to 24-inch lengths. Put meat mixture into a sausage-stuffing machine or into a large pastry bag with a 1/2- to 1-inch tip. Slip casings over end of pastry tip and press meat into casings. If sausage is hard to press into casings, add water to meat mixture to soften it. Makes 2 pounds sausage.

Note: Sausage casings are available from the butcher; extra casings may be frozen.

Braised Lamb Shanks

Lamb is a young sheep, usually between four and twelve months old. Lamb shanks need to be braised in moist heat until tender. Using the same recipe, you can substitute turkey thighs, braising them to tenderness.

4 (3/4-pound) lamb shanks
All-purpose flour
1 tablespoon butter
1 garlic clove, minced or pressed
2 cups water or dry white wine
1 teaspoon salt
1 teaspoon dried leaf thyme
1/4 cup all-purpose flour
1 (8-ounce) can tomato sauce
1 tablespoon chopped fresh parsley
Cooked noodles, rice or mashed potatoes

Dredge lamb shanks in flour until evenly coated. In a large heavy skillet or Dutch oven, heat butter. Add lamb shanks and brown evenly. Add garlic, water or wine, salt and thyme. Cover and simmer over low heat 2 hours or until tender. Remove meat pieces to a warm platter. Stir 1/4 cup flour and tomato sauce into juices in pan. Bring to a boil and stir until thickened and smooth. Return meat to pan; keep warm until ready to serve. Sprinkle with parsley. Serve over noodles, rice or mashed potatoes. Makes 4 servings.

Variation
Braised Turkey Thighs: Substitute 3 pounds (4 pieces) turkey thighs for lamb shanks. Serve with mashed potatoes.

Western Barbecued Leg of Lamb

—— •♦• ——

The idea of barbecue originated in the Western United States before it became popular throughout the country. The Basques, who came from the western Pyrenees regions in France and Spain, have always been known for their barbecue expertise. This is on display at huge community picnics in the Pacific Northwest during which they barbecue lamb basted with lemon juice, herbs and olive oil. In this method, the leg of lamb is butterflied, allowing it to cook quickly on the grill or in a hot oven.

> 1 (5- to 6-pound) leg of lamb, boned, butterflied
> 3/4 cup olive oil
> 1/4 cup fresh lemon juice
> 1/2 cup chopped green onions, including tops
> 3 garlic cloves, minced or pressed
> 2 teaspoons dried leaf rosemary
> 2 teaspoons dried leaf thyme
> 2 teaspoons freshly ground black pepper

Have the butcher prepare the lamb for you. Line a rimmed jelly-roll pan with foil; lay lamb out on it. In a small bowl, combine remaining ingredients; spread mixture over lamb. Marinate in refrigerator overnight. Drain, reserving marinade. Start charcoal. When coals have white edges, place lamb about 3 inches above coals. Brush with marinade while cooking. Cook 35 to 45 minutes or until lamb is crusty on the outside but still pink on the inside. To serve, let cool 5 minutes, then slice on diagonal.

If desired, cook lamb in a preheated 450F (230C) oven 20 minutes or until browned. Reduce heat to 325F (165C) and cook 45 minutes to 1 hour longer or until the meat is pink in center. Makes 6 to 8 servings.

Hunter's Venison

—— ◆ ——

In Montana, this might be made with elk. But this is a basic recipe that can be used for braising almost any cut of venison or large game. To reduce the "gamey" flavor, be sure to trim off all visible fat from the meat. The roasting time varies according to the age of the animal. A young animal is more tender and takes less time to cook.

> **4 to 5 pounds boneless venison, fat trimmed**
> **1/2 cup all-purpose flour**
> **1 teaspoon salt**
> **1/2 teaspoon freshly ground black pepper**
> **Vegetable oil or butter**
> **1 cup red wine, beef broth or water**
> **1 medium-sized onion, quartered**
> **2 carrots, cut into 1-inch pieces**
> **2 celery stalks, cut into 1/2-inch pieces**
> **1 teaspoon *each* dried leaf thyme, basil, oregano**
> **4 juniper berries**
> **1 to 2 cups additional red wine, beef broth or water**
> **1 tablespoon red-currant jelly**
> **1 tablespoon Dijon-style mustard**
> **1/2 cup dairy sour cream**

Preheat oven to 350F (175C). Wash meat and pat dry with paper towels. Combine flour, salt and pepper. Rub meat all over with flour mixture. In a heavy roaster or Dutch oven with a tight-fitting lid, heat enough oil or butter to cover bottom of pan generously. Add meat. Brown over high heat, turning meat constantly. When browned, add 1 cup wine, broth or water, onion, carrots, celery, herbs and juniper berries. Roast, covered, 2 to 3 hours or until meat is fork-tender. Add more liquid, if necessary, to keep meat moist during roasting. Remove meat to a platter; keep warm. Skim off any fat. Taste drippings and adjust seasonings, if necessary. Boil down drippings until they make a thick glaze. Whisk in red-currant jelly, Dijon-mustard and sour cream until blended. Strain and pour over meat on platter. Makes 3 to 4 servings per pound.

Rabbit Pie

◆

If you use wild rather than domestic rabbit in my recipes, the cooking time may be longer to achieve the desired tenderness.

1 (3- to 4-pound) rabbit, cut up
1 small onion, chopped
1 teaspoon dried leaf rosemary
1 teaspoon salt
1/8 teaspoon freshly ground black pepper
About 2 cups water or chicken broth
1/4 cup all-purpose flour
1/4 cup dry sherry or fresh grapefruit juice
1 cup whipping cream

Whole-Wheat Pastry:
1 cup all-purpose flour
1 cup whole-wheat flour
1/2 teaspoon baking powder
1/2 teaspoon salt
3/4 cup shortening or lard
About 2/3 cup milk

Wash rabbit and pat dry with paper towels. Preheat oven to 350F (175C). Arrange rabbit pieces in a shallow 3-quart baking dish. Sprinkle with onion, rosemary, salt and pepper. Add 2 cups water or broth. Bake, covered, 1 to 1-1/2 hours or until rabbit is tender. Remove bones from rabbit, if desired. Measure broth and add water to equal 2 cups. Pour into a skillet and bring to a boil. In a cup, blend flour and sherry or grapefruit juice until smooth. Whisk into broth. Cook, stirring, until thickened and smooth. Add cream. Put rabbit meat into a deep pie dish or casserole. Pour gravy over rabbit. Prepare dough for Whole-Wheat Pastry. Increase oven temperature to 425F (220C). On a lightly floured board, roll out dough to 1/4 inch thick. Cut into strips. Arrange strips over rabbit, making a lattice-work crust. Press edges of crust to edges of dish. Bake 15 to 20 minutes or until crust is browned. Makes 6 servings.

To prepare Whole-Wheat Pastry: In a large bowl, combine flours, baking powder and salt. Using a pastry blender or 2 knives, cut in shortening or lard until mixture resembles coarse crumbs. With a fork, mix in milk. Gently knead just until dough holds together.

Fried Rabbit

—— •◆• ——

Tender rabbit can be fried and served just like chicken. The flavor is much the same.

    1 (3- to 3-1/2-pound) rabbit, cut up
    1/4 cup all-purpose flour
    1-1/2 teaspoons salt
    1 teaspoon paprika
    1/4 teaspoon freshly ground black pepper
    2 to 3 tablespoons vegetable oil or shortening

Wash rabbit and pat dry with paper towels. Combine flour, salt, paprika and pepper in a paper or plastic bag. Drop rabbit pieces, a few at a time, into bag. Shake until each is thoroughly coated with flour mixture. In a large heavy skillet, heat oil or shortening. Add rabbit. Cook over medium heat 10 to 15 minutes, turning pieces to brown evenly. Reduce heat and cover. Cook 30 minutes. Uncover and cook 25 to 35 minutes longer or until meat is tender. Makes 6 servings.

POULTRY

"I wish the Bald Eagle had not been chosen as the representation of our country; he is a bird of bad moral character, like those among men who live by sharpening and robbing, he is generally poor and often very lousy. The turkey is a much more respectable bird, and withal a true original native of America," wrote Benjamin Franklin in a letter dated January 26, 1784.

Early reports of wild turkeys tell of birds as large as 50 pounds! Although the turkey is not mentioned as being on the first Thanksgiving menu in history books, it is safe to assume it was included. As hunters all but obliterated the wild turkey, the bird quickly became domesticated and was soon more abundant and cheaper than chicken.

Ducks and geese were part of the natural bounty of this country. Both have been domesticated, and both are still game for the hunter. Neither are as important as turkey and chicken, although many of the ethnic cultures consider goose the bird for the holiday season.

The domesticated chicken first appeared about 2000 B.C. in India. Chickens were not a common bird in Europe and were considered to be Sunday food. The first chickens were brought by Columbus to America in 1493. An easy bird to raise, the colonists quickly built up their flocks and chickens became an important barnyard fixture.

In the South, they fried chicken in lard and the dish became known as *Southern fried chicken.* Another Southern dish, less well known is Chicken Shortcake made of creamed, cooked chicken served between squares of cornbread which had been sliced in half like a hot biscuit. Chicken pot pies originated in New England in the 1800's as did chicken salad.

The Pennsylvania Dutch had folklore about talking cows on Christmas Eve, but chicken and other members of the poultry family did not find themselves subjects of such endearing tales. Chicken was always considered good eating as you will find in the following recipes, and there were plenty of them for Sunday and holiday meals.

Southern Fried Chicken with Cream Gravy

·◆·

Typical of foods that are cooked by nearly every family in an area, there are many variations to this Southern classic. Some prefer to add Tabasco sauce to the chicken. Some dip the chicken in milk instead of water. All dip the chicken pieces in flour, but some prefer to brown them in lard, partly lard, oil, or bacon drippings. In some recipes the chicken is cooked entirely in the fat. In others it is simply browned, then placed on a baking sheet and finished off in a low oven. Gravy is made from the drippings in the pan. Some cooks prefer to use milk, some use water, and in our variation we use a combination of chicken broth and cream.

> **1 (2-1/2-pound) frying chicken, cut up**
> **1 teaspoon salt**
> **1 cup all-purpose flour**
> **1 cup fat (all lard or 1/2 lard, 1/2 vegetable oil or shortening)**
> **2 tablespoons all-purpose flour**
> **1 cup chicken broth**
> **About 1/2 cup whipping cream**
> **Salt and freshly ground black pepper to taste**

Wash chicken and pat dry with paper towels. Sprinkle with 1 teaspoon salt. Put 1 cup flour in a paper or plastic bag. Drop chicken pieces, 2 at a time, into bag. Shake until each piece is thoroughly coated with flour. Lay chicken on a sheet of waxed paper. Preheat oven to 300F (150C). In a large heavy skillet, heat fat. Fat should be 1/4 inch deep. Reduce heat to medium-high. Add legs and thighs, skin-side down. Fat should sizzle when chicken is added, but should not be so hot that chicken burns. Brown legs and thighs 7 to 8 minutes or until deep brown on 1 side. Turn and brown on second side, about 7 minutes. Line a baking sheet with brown paper. Remove chicken to baking sheet. Place in oven while you continue browning remaining chicken pieces. Bake chicken 30 minutes after last pieces have been browned. Meanwhile, pour off all but 2 tablespoons fat from skillet. Add 2 tablespoons flour and stir until combined. Whisk in chicken broth and cream. Bring to a boil. Cook, stirring, until gravy is thickened and smooth. If it is too thick, stir in a little more cream to thin. Strain gravy through a fine sieve, if desired. Taste and adjust seasoning, if necessary. Place fried chicken on a warm serving platter. Serve gravy with chicken. Makes 4 servings.

Oven-Fried Chicken

In the days of the Old West, the usual question from the waitress at an inn was, "What will you have? Brown meal and common doings, or white wheat and chicken fixings?" Translated that is, "Will you have pork and brown bread or white bread and fried chicken?" (Frederick Marryat, *A Diary in America*, 1839.)

> 1 (2-1/2- to 3-pound) frying chicken, cut up
> Salt and freshly ground black pepper to taste
> 1/4 cup melted butter
> 3 cups corn flakes

Preheat oven to 375F (190C). Wash chicken and pat dry with paper towels. Sprinkle with salt and pepper. Brush each piece of chicken with melted butter. Crush corn flakes; put on a plate. Roll chicken pieces in corn flakes. Place chicken, skin-side up, in a shallow baking pan. Bake 50 minutes or until chicken is tender and golden. Makes 6 servings.

Skillet-Fried Chicken

In the South, the first thought for a quick and easy dinner is to "fry up a chicken." This is how it is done.

> 1 (2-1/2 to 3-pound) frying chicken, cut up
> 1/4 cup all-purpose flour
> 1-1/2 teaspoons salt
> 1 teaspoon paprika
> 1/4 teaspoon freshly ground black pepper
> 2 to 3 tablespoons vegetable oil or shortening

Wash chicken and pat dry with paper towels. In a paper or plastic bag, combine flour, salt, paprika and pepper. Drop chicken pieces, 2 at a time, into bag. Shake until each piece is thoroughly coated with flour. In a large heavy skillet, heat oil or shortening. Add chicken. Cook over medium heat 10 to 15 minutes, turning pieces to brown evenly. Reduce heat and cover. Cook 30 minutes. Uncover and cook 10 to 15 minutes longer. Chicken is done when juices run clear when pierced with a fork. Makes 6 servings.

Chicken & Dumplings

◆

This is probably one of the favorite original "one-pot meals" in American cooking. Dumpling dough or batter bakes right on top of the stewed chicken in a covered pot.

What is considered a "dumpling" is different from one area of the country to another. Dumplings may take the form of a fresh noodle, spatzle, as in Hungarian and German cuisine, or a dumpling may be made of a dough similar to baking-powder biscuits as in this recipe.

It is important when making dumplings leavened with baking powder that you cover the pot and allow the dumplings to steam for 15 minutes without lifting the lid or the dumplings will be doughy rather than light and fluffy.

1 (3-1/2-pound) chicken, cut up
1-1/2 quarts water
Salt and freshly ground black pepper to taste
1 small onion, quartered
1 small carrot, cut into chunks
2 celery stalks with leaves, cut into chunks
3 tablespoons butter or chicken fat
1/4 cup all-purpose flour
1/8 teaspoon paprika
1/2 cup half and half
White pepper to taste
Chopped fresh parsley

Dumplings:
1-1/2 cups all-purpose flour
1/2 teaspoon salt
3 teaspoons baking powder
1 tablespoon melted shortening
1/3 cup milk

Wash chicken and pat dry with paper towels. Place chicken in a large pot. Add water, salt, black pepper, onion, carrot and celery. Simmer, covered, 45 minutes to 1 hour or until chicken is tender. Remove from broth; strain and reserve broth. Place chicken on a rack in a bowl; cool enough to handle. Remove and discard skin and bones from chicken. Dice meat; refrigerate. In a large heavy saucepan, heat butter or chicken fat. Stir in flour and paprika. Gradually add 3 cups reserved chicken broth, stirring until thickened and smooth. Cook 2 minutes. Add half and half and white pepper. Taste and adjust seasoning, if necessary. Return chicken to sauce. Prepare Dumplings. Dip a teaspoon into cold water, then spoon teaspoonfuls of batter on top of simmering chicken mixture. Cook, covered, 15 minutes without lifting lid. Sprinkle with parsley and serve immediately. Makes 6 servings.
To prepare Dumplings: In a medium-sized bowl, combine flour, salt and baking powder. Blend in shortening and milk; mix well.

Paprika Chicken

◆

In the mid-1800s, Chicago, Milwaukee, St. Louis, Cincinnati and other smaller cities of the Midwest were where the Germans, Austrians, Hungarians and Bohemians settled their own little neighborhoods. Paprika and Pilsener, breweries and pastry shops, knackwurst, coffeecakes, pretzels and potato dumplings became trademarks of these cities. Although the cuisines of the countries are different, they also overlap in many ways. Hungarian women were great cooks and were known for their stuffed cabbage, goulash, chicken and veal "paprikash," and all kinds of strudels. Chicken, an expensive dish of the past, is now our most abundant fowl. Paprika Chicken is served with a freshly made noodle called *spatzle*.

 1 (2-1/2- to 3-pound) frying chicken, cut up
 Salt and freshly ground black pepper to taste
 1/4 cup butter
 1 garlic clove, mashed
 1 small onion, chopped
 1/4 cup Hungarian sweet paprika
 3 tablespoons tomato paste
 1-1/2 cups chicken broth
 1 green bell pepper, cut into 1-inch strips
 1/2 cup dairy sour cream
 Spatzle, page 71

Wash chicken and pat dry with paper towels. Sprinkle chicken with salt and pepper. In a heavy Dutch oven or deep skillet, heat butter. Add chicken pieces, a few at a time, and starting with legs and thighs. Brown over medium heat on all sides. Add garlic as you brown chicken. Drain off excess fat. Add onion, paprika, tomato paste and chicken broth. Cook, covered, over low heat 25 to 30 minutes or until chicken is tender. Add green pepper. Simmer, uncovered, 10 minutes longer. Degrease drippings again, if necessary. Remove chicken to a warm platter. Stir sour cream into pan juices. Pour over chicken. Serve over warm Spatzle. Makes 4 servings.

Smothered Chicken with Mushrooms

Sunday chicken dinner on the farm was often prepared this way. The chicken pieces are first browned in butter and oil. The thickened sauce starts with the pan drippings and takes just a couple of minutes to make. Then it is poured over the chicken which finishes its cooking in the oven. The result is chicken that's succulent and juicy, baked beneath a mushroom sauce. When canned soups arrived on the American scene, cooks began using cream of mushroom soup and the taste was never the same!

1 (2-1/2- to 3-pound) frying chicken, cut up
Salt and freshly ground black pepper to taste
1 tablespoon butter
2 tablespoons vegetable oil
1 small onion, chopped
1/2 pound fresh mushrooms, sliced
3 tablespoons all-purpose flour
1-1/2 cups chicken broth
1/2 cup whipping cream or milk
Chopped fresh parsley

Preheat oven to 350F (175C). Wash chicken and pat dry with paper towels. Pull off any excess fat from chicken. To further reduce caloric count, remove skin. Sprinkle pieces with salt and pepper. In a large heavy skillet, heat butter and oil over high heat. Add chicken, skin-side down. Brown on 1 side then turn over. Remove from skillet to a shallow casserole, laying chicken in a single layer. Pour off all but 2 tablespoons fat from skillet. Add onion and mushrooms to skillet. Sauté over medium heat 5 minutes, stirring occasionally. Stir in flour, then chicken broth, whisking until sauce is thickened. Simmer 3 minutes. Add cream or milk. Pour sauce over chicken in casserole. Bake, covered, 20 minutes. Remove cover and continue baking 30 minutes longer or until chicken is tender but not falling apart. Before serving, spoon off excess surface fat and spoon pan gravy over chicken. Sprinkle with parsley. Makes 4 servings.

Cape Cod Chicken Pie

•◆•

From all outward appearances, this could as well be an apple pie. It was and still is, a custom to bake boned well-seasoned chicken between two pastry crusts. Gravy is spooned over each wedge of pie at the table. Chicken pie has always been a favorite at Grange suppers and other community meals. Sometimes the pies were baked with a lattice-work crust on top. Cranberry sauce, made with chopped raw berries and chopped raw orange is often served with the pie.

1 (5-pound) stewing chicken
1-1/2 quarts water
2 teaspoons salt
1 small onion, quartered
1 carrot, cut into chunks
1 celery stalk
Dough for Basic Foolproof Lard Crust, page 187
1/2 cup all-purpose flour
1/2 teaspoon onion salt
1/2 teaspoon celery salt
Salt and freshly ground black pepper to taste

Place chicken in a large pot. Add water, 2 teaspoons salt, onion, carrot and celery. Simmer, covered, 45 minutes to 1 hour or until chicken is tender. Remove from broth; strain and reserve broth. Place chicken on a rack in a bowl; cool enough to handle. Prepare dough and refrigerate 30 minutes before rolling out. Remove and discard skin and bones from chicken. Cut meat into small pieces; refrigerate. In a cup, blend flour, onion salt, celery salt, salt, pepper and 1/2 cup reserved chicken broth until smooth. In a large heavy saucepan, bring 3 cups chicken broth to a boil. Add flour mixture, beating with a whisk to prevent lumping. Cook, stirring, over medium heat, until mixture is thickened and smooth. Add chicken. Preheat oven to 400F (205C). On a lightly floured board, roll out half of dough to fit a 9-inch, deep-dish, pie pan. Line pan with dough. Fill with chicken mixture. Roll out remaining dough for top crust. Cover chicken mixture with top crust. Seal and flute edges. Make several slits for steam to escape around edge of top crust. Bake 45 minutes or until browned. Makes 6 to 8 servings.

Note: Remaining broth may be frozen or used to make a gravy to serve with the pie.

Maryland Sweet & Sour Chicken Salad

A simple chicken salad can be the main dish for a picnic, wedding reception or almost any kind of occasion where a number of friends and family gather for an event. This salad will serve about 20 people.

3 (3-pound) frying chickens, cut up
1/4 cup sugar
2 teaspoons all-purpose flour
1-1/2 teaspoons salt
3 eggs
1 teaspoon Dijon-style mustard
1 cup water
1-1/4 cups cider vinegar
2 teaspoons butter
6 cups diced celery
1-1/2 cups mayonnaise
Salt and freshly ground black pepper to taste

Place chicken in a large pot. Add boiling water to cover. Simmer, covered, 45 minutes to 1 hour or until chicken is tender. Cool chicken in broth. When cool enough to handle, remove and discard skin and bones from chicken. Cut meat into bite-sized pieces; refrigerate. In a medium-sized heavy saucepan, combine sugar, flour and 1-1/2 teaspoons salt. Add eggs and mustard. Whisk until blended. Add water and vinegar. Place over low heat. Cook 10 minutes over low heat, whisking until smooth and about the consistency of whipping cream. Remove from heat; whisk in butter. Cool 5 to 10 minutes. Pour dressing over chicken. Marinate in refrigerator at least 4 hours, preferably overnight. Add celery, mayonnaise, salt and pepper to chicken mixture. Toss well and serve. Makes 18 to 20 servings.

Chicken Jambalaya Creole

––––––––––––––––––––––––––– ◆ –––––––––––––––––––––––––––

A "Creole" according to definition, is a person who is born in the region but is of European ancestry and continues to maintain some of the customs and languages of the mother country. Creole and Cajun cuisines of Louisiana are a mixture of French, Native American Indian, Spanish, German and African cookery. French is the major influence. The Spanish developed the spicy nature of the dishes by using red pepper and added the technique of making a hot red-pepper sauce. *Jambalaya* is a word that was first published in 1872. It is believed that the name comes from the Spanish word for ham, *jamon,* and the word *balayez* in the dialect of Louisiana, meaning to "mix things together." Although ham was the primary ingredient in the jambalayas of the 1800s, it is often not included in recipes today. Jambalaya can be made with beef, pork, chicken, shrimp, oysters, crayfish, alone or in any combination. It includes onions, celery, bell pepper, garlic, tomatoes and spices as well as rice. Spiciness is negotiable, but Creole cooking tends to be a little less spicy than Cajun.

> 1 (5-pound) stewing chicken, cut up
> 2 quarts water
> 4 to 5 sprigs fresh thyme, marjoram or parsley
> 2 bay leaves
> Salt, red (cayenne) pepper and freshly grated nutmeg to taste
> 1/4 cup butter
> 2 garlic cloves, minced or pressed
> 2 large onions, sliced lengthwise
> 3 celery stalks, cut julienne
> 1 large green bell pepper, sliced
> 1 cup uncooked long-grain rice
> 1 (15- to 16-ounce) can stewed tomatoes
> 1 cup buttered fresh bread crumbs
> Chopped fresh parsley

Place chicken in a large pot. Add water, fresh herb sprigs and bay leaves. Simmer, covered, 45 minutes to 1 hour or until chicken is tender. Remove from broth; strain broth. Return broth to pot and boil down until it measure 3 cups. Remove and discard skin and bones from chicken. Pull meat into large shreds; refrigerate. Preheat oven to 350F (175C). Grease a 3-quart casserole. Taste broth and add salt, red pepper and nutmeg. In a large skillet, heat butter. Add garlic, onions, celery and green pepper. Sauté 5 minutes, stirring constantly, until vegetables are limp but not browned. Add rice, tomatoes and chicken. Bake, covered, 45 minutes or until rice is tender. Top with buttered bread crumbs. Bake, covered, 15 minutes longer. Sprinkle with chopped parsley. Makes 8 servings.

Note: To make buttered bread crumbs, combine 1 cup soft bread crumbs and 3 to 4 tablespoons melted butter in a skillet. Sauté until bread crumbs are coated with butter and lightly browned.

Georgia Country Captain

Georgians claim this dish as their own. According to legend, a mysterious captain drifted into Savannah through involvement in the spice trade and entrusted this recipe to his Southern friends.

1 (5-pound) stewing chicken
2 quarts water
4 to 5 fresh sprigs thyme or marjoram
3 tablespoons olive oil
2 medium-sized onions, chopped
1 garlic clove, minced or pressed
1 green bell pepper, chopped
2 (16-ounce) cans whole tomatoes, or 1 quart home-canned
   tomatoes
2 to 6 teaspoons curry powder
1 teaspoon *each* ground thyme, salt and sugar
1/8 teaspoon red (cayenne) pepper
1/2 cup dried currants
1 cup blanched whole almonds
Additional currants
Cooked brown or wild rice
Chopped peanuts
Shredded coconut
Chutney, purchased or homemade

Place chicken in a large pot. Add water and fresh herb sprigs. Simmer, covered, 45 minutes to 1 hour or until chicken is tender. Remove from broth; strain broth. Return broth to pot and boil down until it measure 3 cups. Remove and discard skin and bones from chicken. Pull meat into large shreds; refrigerate. Preheat oven to 350F (175C). In a large heavy skillet, heat oil. Add onions, garlic and green pepper. Sauté about 5 minutes or until soft. Add tomatoes with juice. Cook 5 minutes. Stir in curry powder, ground thyme, salt, sugar, red pepper and 1/2 cup currants. Simmer 10 minutes. Add chicken. Turn into a 3-quart casserole. Bake, uncovered, 45 minutes or until heated through. Sprinkle with almonds and additional currants. Serve over cooked rice. Add chopped peanuts, coconut and chutney to each individual serving. Makes 6 to 8 servings.

Note: As with many recipes where chicken is cooked and then boned, the work can be done ahead in stages and the components of the dish assembled and reheated at serving time.

Chicken Livers & Wild Rice

—— ·◆· ——

Wild rice is not really a rice but is the seed of an aquatic wild grass which grows in marshy northern areas, particularly in northern Minnesota and Canada. It is a food that is still important in the diet of Native Americans and is grown and harvested either the "old-fashioned Indian way," or is grown in paddies and mechanically harvested.

2/3 cup uncooked wild rice
2-1/2 cups water
1/2 teaspoon salt
1/2 cup butter
1 medium-sized onion, minced
1/2 pound fresh (domestic or wild) mushrooms, sliced
1 green bell pepper, minced
1 pound chicken livers, cleaned, halved
2 to 3 tablespoons all-purpose flour
1 teaspoon salt
1/4 teaspoon freshly ground black pepper

Wash rice in 3 changes of hot tap water; drain. Place in a 2-quart saucepan. Add water and 1/2 teaspoon salt. Bring to a boil. Cover and reduce heat to low. Simmer 35 to 40 minutes or until rice is tender but not mushy. Drain off any excess water. In a large heavy skillet, heat 2 tablespoons butter. Add onion, mushrooms and green pepper. Sauté 5 minutes or until vegetables are soft. Stir in cooked rice. Keep warm until ready to serve. Remove onto a warm serving platter if you need to use same skillet for cooking chicken livers. In heavy skillet, heat remaining butter over medium-high heat. Dust chicken livers on all sides with flour. Add to hot butter. Cook quickly until browned but not overdone. Sprinkle with salt and black pepper. Serve hot chicken livers over wild-rice mixture. Makes 6 main-dish servings or 8 to 12 first-course servings.

Roast Goose with Mashed-Potato Dressing

—————————————— · ◆ · ——————————————

The early colonists were fed from the generous supply of nature. Part of that supply was a bountiful selection of birds and fowl. Geese and ducks covered coastal waters, lakes and rivers during the autumn migratory season making them a perfect choice for the Thanksgiving and Christmas meals. Today, our choice is most likely a domesticated goose, grown for consumption. Because there is so much fat that drains off the goose, it is better to bake a dressing in a separate dish rather than to stuff the bird.

> 1 (8- to 9-pound) goose
> 1 lemon, cut in half
> 2 garlic cloves, minced or pressed
> 2 teaspoons coarse kosher-style salt
> Applesauce
>
> *Mashed-Potato Dressing:*
> 2 cups hot mashed potatoes
> 1-1/2 cups fresh whole-wheat bread crumbs
> 1 medium-sized onion, chopped
> 2 eggs
> 1 teaspoon salt
> 1 teaspoon dried sage
> 1/2 cup chopped celery leaves
> 1/4 cup chopped fresh parsley

Preheat oven to 350F (175C). Thaw goose if frozen. Wash inside and out and pat dry with paper towels. Rub goose with cut lemon. Place lemon halves inside cavity of goose. Mix garlic and salt; rub over surface of goose. Place on a rack in a roasting pan. Using a fork, pierce skin over breast of goose in several places. Roast goose 20 to 25 minutes per pound. Pierce skin again during cooking to release fat into pan beneath. Meanwhile, prepare Mashed-Potato Dressing. Place in oven 1 hour before goose is done. Bake 45 minutes, then remove cover. Bake dressing 15 minutes longer. Serve goose with dressing and applesauce. Makes 6 servings.
To prepare Mashed-Potato Dressing: In a large bowl, combine mashed potatoes, bread crumbs, onion, eggs, salt, sage, celery leaves and parsley. Turn into a 1-quart baking dish; cover.

Thanksgiving Roasted Turkey

·◆·

The Thanksgiving feast has the tradition of being a shared meal. When they gathered together to celebrate the harvest, the Indians and Pilgrims brought with them gifts from nature's bounty, pumpkins, squash, fowl and berries. This started a warm tradition for a uniquely American holiday.

The Thanksgiving dinner goes beyond the boundaries of a potluck dinner. Nothing is left to luck. The meal is a rich reminder of our roots. The foods tend to be traditional, with the host usually supplying the turkey and guests contributing interesting side dishes and desserts. Although variations of the classic dishes are allowed, certain key ingredients must be included in the traditional Thanksgiving menu. The obligatory ingredients are cranberries, sweet potatoes and pumpkin.

Allow 1 pound of turkey per serving when you purchase your turkey. If you select a frozen turkey, thaw it in the refrigerator for 2 to 3 days. Then proceed with the recipe. It will take 24 hours for every 5 pounds of turkey to thaw. For quick thawing, place in the sink and cover with cold water. Change water frequently and allow 30 minutes per pound of turkey for thawing. Remove neck and giblets from cavities. Rinse turkey with cold water; drain and pat dry with paper towels. Stuff neck cavity loosely with your favorite stuffing. Fasten neck skin with a skewer. Stuff body cavity loosely. Return legs to hock lock or cross drumsticks and tie together. Turn wing tips onto back of turkey. Place, breast-side up, on a rack in a shallow roasting pan or roaster. Brush entire bird with oil. Cover loosely with a "tent" of light-weight foil, or roast bird without foil until desired browness, then cover with foil tent. Roast in a 325F (165C) oven until a meat thermometer, inserted in the thigh registers 180F (80C).

Remove turkey to a large, warm, serving platter; cover loosely with foil. Skim fat from pan juices. Pour juices into a jug; you should have about 4 cups. Set roasting pan over 2 burners on stove. Slowly stir and brown 1/2 cup flour in pan over low to medium heat. Gradually whisk in pan juices, stirring constantly, until gravy is thickened and smooth. Add salt and pepper to taste and cream, if desired. If gravy has lumps, process briefly in a blender.

Approximate Roasting Time in a 325F (165C) Oven

Ready-to-cook Weight	Approximate Cooking Time
6 to 8 pounds	2-1/2 to 3 hours
8 to 12 pounds	3 to 3-1/2 hours
12 to 16 pounds	3-1/2 to 4-1/2 hours
16 to 20 pounds	4-1/4 to 5 hours
20 to 24 pounds	5 to 6 hours

Corn-Bread Stuffing

⸻ ◆ ⸻

This classic stuffing for the Thanksgiving turkey starts with a recipe for corn bread. The sausage was added as a way to stretch the servings of turkey; it can be omitted.

> **1-1/2 cups cornmeal**
> **2 cups all-purpose flour**
> **2 tablespoons sugar**
> **1 teaspoon salt**
> **4 teaspoons baking powder**
> **2 eggs**
> **1 pint milk (2 cups)**
> **1/4 cup melted butter**
> **1 pound seasoned, bulk-type, breakfast sausage**
> **2 tablespoons bacon fat**
> **4 medium-sized onions, finely chopped**
> **4 celery stalks, finely chopped**
> **1/2 teaspoon dried sage**
> **1/2 teaspoon dried leaf thyme**
> **1 teaspoon salt**
> **Dash of freshly ground black pepper**

Preheat oven to 450F (230C). Grease a 13" x 9" baking pan. In a large bowl, combine cornmeal, flour, sugar, 1 teaspoon salt and baking powder. Stir in eggs, milk and melted butter until blended. Spread in greased baking pan. Bake 30 minutes. Cool. Crumble cooled corn bread. In a medium-sized skillet, brown sausage over low heat until cooked through, breaking it into pieces with a fork. Add crumbled corn bread; remove from heat. In another skillet, heat bacon fat. Add onions and celery. Sauté until tender. Add to corn bread mixture. Add remaining seasonings. Use mixture to stuff a 12- to 15-pound turkey.

Turkey Breast with Country-Style Gravy

The turkey "tenderloin" is the boneless meat which separates from the turkey breast and has a silver membrane running through it. Turkey tenderloins are available in the poultry section of fresh-meat counters at supermarkets today. When the silver is removed, the meat will separate into two slender portions, about 3 to 4 ounces each. If you wish, you may cut boneless turkey breast into individual-sized pieces (about 4 ounces each) for this recipe. This cut of turkey cooks quickly so be careful not to overcook it or it will be dry. For a holiday buffet, serve this with Wild Rice & Pecan Dressing, page 64.

1 to 1-1/2 pounds turkey breast tenderloin
1/4 cup fresh lemon juice
Salt and freshly ground black pepper to taste
2 tablespoons butter
1 tablespoon olive oil
1/2 cup chicken broth
1/2 pint whipping cream (1 cup)

Remove silver membrane from turkey tenderloins; in so doing you will cut each piece into 2 long narrow pieces. Brush with 1 tablespoon lemon juice and sprinkle with salt and pepper. In a large heavy skillet, heat butter and oil. Add turkey. Cook over medium heat 10 to 15 minutes or until just cooked through, turning often. Do not overcook meat or it will be dry. Remove and keep warm. Add remaining lemon juice and chicken broth to skillet. Bring to a boil; scrape up brownings. Add cream. Boil until thickened and reduced by about half. Add salt and pepper. Add turkey to sauce. Cook only until heated to serving temperature. Makes 4 servings.

✦ FISH & SEAFOOD ✦

Between the "sea and shining sea" the early settlers in America counted fish and seafood in with the native bounty. Bass, trout, perch, chub, sturgeon (some 12 feet long) were there for the taking in fresh waters. Along the seashore were clams, oysters, scallops, mussels and other shellfish. There were giant crabs and lobsters large enough to feed four persons each. In historic books, there are reports of lobsters caught that were 6 feet long!

The gift of the Algonquin Indians to New England was the clambake which became a colorful seaside meal. Native Americans were experts at community meals. In the Great Lakes region, the "fish boil" was introduced by the Chippewas to the locals. Today, inns and restaurants in northern Wisconsin and Minnesota feature this meal of whitefish and potatoes cooked in large pots over an open fire.

Fishing today is a weekend ritual in many rural areas of America. "Up north" where we live, the opening of fishing season which is usually on Mother's Day, leaves Mom home, unless she is a fisher lady, to munch on tuna-fish sandwiches. The high point of the day occurs when the fishermen return home with the catch. There is nothing in the world tastier than freshly caught fish, quickly cooked in butter!

Although the fisher-person often is not the fisher-cook, the most common mistake made in cooking fish is to overcook it. Fish that is cooked too much is dry and fishy tasting. A rule of thumb is that fish, either whole or filleted, laid on its side and measured, should be cooked 10 minutes per inch of thickness, whether it is poached, fried or broiled. Baked fish may take longer depending on the oven temperature.

Catfish Fillets Sautéed in Garlic Butter

Catfish has no bones and a rather compact flesh so it takes about twice as long to cook in a pan as any other fish. Offer lemon wedges to squeeze over the fillets. To make an authentic meal, serve with steamed mixed greens such as collard greens or kale.

> 1 pound catfish fillets
> All-purpose flour
> 1/4 cup unsalted butter
> 1/4 cup olive oil
> 2 garlic cloves, minced or pressed
> Lemon wedges

Rinse catfish in cold water and pat dry with paper towels. With a sharp knife, cut fillets lengthwise along center to make long thin pieces. Dust with flour. In a heavy skillet, heat butter and olive oil. Add garlic. Sauté 1 minute. Add fish fillets. Sauté over medium-high heat about 10 minutes or until fish is cooked through. Serve immediately with lemon wedges. Makes 4 servings.

Fried Catfish

Catfish is the fish with a thick skin and no scales. At its large mouth it has whisker-like barbels, similar to a cat's whiskers. Catfish has always been popular in the South. Along the Great River Road, which runs beside the Mississippi river from northern Minnesota to Southern Louisiana, there are restaurants that specialize in crusty, deep-fried catfish. Serve with Hush Puppies, page 144.

> 1 pound catfish fillets
> 1 egg, beaten
> 1 cup milk
> 1/2 cup water
> 1/2 cup prepared mustard
> 1 garlic clove, minced or pressed
> Salt and red (cayenne) pepper to taste
> 1 cup yellow cornmeal
> 1 cup yellow corn flour (masa is suitable)
> Vegetable oil

Rinse catfish in cold water and pat dry with paper towels. With a sharp knife, cut fillets lengthwise along center to make long thin pieces. In a shallow bowl, mix egg, milk and water. Add fish to milk mixture. In another bowl, blend mustard and garlic. Drain fish. Roll in mustard mixture. Sprinkle with salt and red pepper. In another bowl, combine cornmeal and corn flour. Roll fish in cornmeal mixture until well-coated. Heat oil to 375F (190C) or until a 1-inch cube of bread turns golden brown in 50 seconds. Deep-fry fish in oil until golden, 3 to 5 minutes, depending on size of fish. Drain on paper towels and serve immediately. Makes about 4 servings.

Baked Walleye with Lemon & Cream

· ◆ ·

Use a pair of pliers to pluck out the small bones that stick out on the ridge of the fillets before assembling this dish.

1 medium (1-1/2-pound) walleye, trout, or whitefish, filleted
3 bacon slices, chopped
1 small onion, minced
1/2 cup whipping cream
3 tablespoons fresh lemon juice
1/2 teaspoon Dijon-style mustard
1 tablespoon chopped fresh parsley
1/2 cup (2 ounces) shredded sharp Cheddar cheese
2 tablespoons fine dry bread crumbs

Lightly grease a shallow baking dish. Preheat oven to 375F (190C). Rinse fish in cold water and pat dry with paper towels. Place 1 fillet, skin-side down, in greased baking dish. In a heavy skillet, cook bacon until crisp. Add onion. Sauté 2 minutes. Drain excess fat from skillet. Add cream. Bring to a rolling boil; boil 1 minute. Add lemon juice, mustard and parsley. Spoon half of mixture over fish in baking dish. Top with second fillet, skin-side up. Spoon remaining mixture over top of fish. Sprinkle with cheese and bread crumbs. Bake 25 minutes or until fish flakes. Serve hot. Makes 4 servings.

Boston Scrod

· ◆ ·

Newcomers to the Boston area wonder what kind of fish this is. Scrod is the baby haddock or cod which weighs 2-1/2 pounds or less. Originally, the definition applied to any young fish that was prepared for "planking," that is, broiling on a wooden plank.

1 (2-1/2-pound) baby haddock or cod
Salt and freshly ground black pepper to taste
About 1/4 cup melted butter or vegetable oil
1/2 to 1 cup fresh bread crumbs
Additional melted butter
Fresh lemon juice

Preheat broiler. Set the rack at highest level under broiler. Clean fish, removing head, tail and backbone and leaving all skin intact so entire fish can be opened up flat. Rinse fish in cold water and pat dry with paper towels. Sprinkle with salt and pepper. Dip in about 1/4 cup melted butter or oil. Roll in fresh bread crumbs. Place on broiler rack or plank, flesh-side up; slip under broiler. Broil 4 to 5 minutes or until fish is about half-cooked. Turn over and broil, skin-side up, until skin is lightly browned. Turn again so flesh side is up and drizzle with additional melted butter; sprinkle with lemon juice. Serve immediately. Makes 3 to 4 servings.

Codfish Balls with Fresh-Tomato Sauce

Codfish is one of the oldest of American foods. The Pilgrim Fathers practically lived on it. Each year as cold weather approached, they put away stores of meaty cod, carefully preserved with salt. Codfish balls were a favorite in the early days of the United States Senate where Senator George Frisbie Hoar rose during a debate on a pure-food bill to praise "the exquisite flavor of the codfish, salted, made into balls, and eaten on a Sunday morning by a person whose theology is sound, and who believes in the five points of Calvinism."

Fresh-Tomato Sauce, opposite
1/2 pound shredded salt codfish
1 whole egg
1 egg yolk
2 cups mashed potatoes
1-1/2 tablespoons whipping cream
1 tablespoon finely chopped fresh parsley
1 tablespoon finely chopped chives
1 teaspoon grated onion
1/8 teaspoon *each* dried leaf thyme, ground nutmeg and red
    (cayenne) pepper
Hot fat
Broiled bacon slices

Prepare Fresh-Tomato Sauce; set aside. Soak and drain codfish according to package directions. In a large bowl, beat egg and egg yolk until foamy. Add fish and mashed potatoes, blending thoroughly. Add cream, parsley, chives, onion, thyme, nutmeg and red pepper. In a deep heavy skillet, heat fat to 360F (180C) or until a 1-inch cube of bread turns golden brown in 60 seconds. Drop codfish mixture by tablespoons into hot fat. Fry until brown, turning once. Drain well. Serve with broiled bacon slices and Fresh-Tomato Sauce. Makes 4 servings.

Fresh-Tomato Sauce

This sauce is also delicious with poached chicken breasts.

> **3 tablespoons olive oil**
> **1 garlic clove**
> **1 large Bermuda onion, chopped**
> **1/2 large green bell pepper, chopped**
> **1/2 small carrot, chopped**
> **1 quart chopped fresh tomatoes**
> **1 large bay leaf**
> **4 sprigs green celery tops**
> **1 small thyme sprig or 1 teaspoon dried leaf thyme**
> **Salt and freshly ground black pepper to taste**

In a large saucepan, heat oil. Add garlic, onion, green pepper and carrot. Sauté 4 minutes, stirring constantly, until onion begins to brown lightly. Add tomatoes, bay leaf, celery, thyme, salt and black pepper. Simmer slowly 40 minutes. Puree in a blender or food processor fitted with the steel blade. Makes 4 cups.

Baked Whole Salmon, Coho Salmon or Trout

"Fishin'" is probably the first sport a country kid learns. What is caught depends on where one lives. Around the Great Lakes, it is possible to fish off tributaries and rocky ledges to land big, salmon-like trout. The cooking of any variety of fish is the same if the sizes are the same.

> **1 whole 3- to 5-pound salmon, Coho salmon or Lake Superior**
> **trout**
> **Salt and freshly ground black pepper to taste**
> **Butter**
> **Celery tops**
> **Curled parsley**

Preheat oven to 350F (175C). Wash fish inside and out. Dry cavity and outside with paper towels. Sprinkle inside and out with salt and pepper. Place on a rack over a shallow baking pan. Dot with bits of butter. Cover with waxed paper or parchment paper. Bake, uncovered, 45 minutes to 1 hour or until flesh flakes when probed with a fork. Garnish with celery tops and curled parsley. Makes 4 servings.

New England Clambake

—— ◆ ——

"It was a real nice clambake" sang the chorus in Rodgers & Hammerstein's *Carousel*. "Clambake" is a Northeast seaside rite and tradition as much as a beef barbecue is in Texas, a fish fry in the South or a luau in Hawaii. This is a colorful seaside party meal originated by the Indians who served only fish, corn and clams. They passed on their techniques to the early settlers, and to this day there is little that has changed in the affair.

To figure on amounts, count 1 piece of vegetable per person, 10 to 12 clams each, and 1 lobster for every 3 to 4 persons. Obviously, you need many helpers and one "bakemaster" to succeed. Here is a description of the pit for a clambake adapted from Nell Nichol's superb classic *Good Home Cooking Across The USA*, 1952 Iowa State College Press.

"The pit must be dug 4 by 6 feet and 9 inches deep. It is filled with rocks the size of cabbages until it is even to the ground. On top of that are laid two layers of firewood, then a layer of stones the size of cabbages. On top of this go two more layers of firewood and the layering is repeated until the pit is 3 to 4 feet high. The wood is ignited and should burn down completely. This would take 2 hours or more. The wood and embers are raked away and the hot stones are covered with 6 to 8 inches of seaweed. On top of that are layered first clams then sweet potatoes and onions, fish wrapped in individual paper bags, sausages or frankfurters wrapped in paper bags, corn in the husk, and 65 lobsters tied in cheesecloth squares. More clams go over the top along with 4 to 6 inches more of seaweed. Finally the whole thing is covered with a piece of canvas large enough to extend over the ground and fasten down tightly around the edges with rocks to prevent the escape of steam. This is allowed to steam for 1 hour."

To serve the clambake, the canvas and seaweed are removed. The aromas waft, and it is time to eat. Accompanying the contents of the pit, there are usually crisp cucumbers and sliced tomatoes, buttered Boston brown and white breads, and hot clam broth to sip from mugs. The necessary condiments are melted butter and pepper sauce or vinegar.

New England Scalloped Oysters

While many New Englanders serve oyster stew for Christmas Eve and the "watch party" on New Year's Eve, scalloped oysters might also be the "pièce de résistance" of the meal. In the famous dish, the oysters must not be more than two layers deep. Before baking, they are layered with crumbs mixed with butter, salt and pepper, and whole milk or cream is poured over along with a touch of sherry.

1/4 cup butter
2 cups coarsely crushed saltines (about 24 crackers)
1/2 cup chopped fresh parsley
Dash of salt and freshly ground black pepper
1 pint (about 24) fresh shucked oysters with liquor
1/2 cup half and half
1 tablespoon sherry
1 teaspoon Worcestershire sauce

Preheat oven to 350F (175C). In a small saucepan, heat butter. Remove from heat and stir in cracker crumbs, parsley, salt and pepper. Drain and reserve 1/4 cup liquor from oysters. Sprinkle one-third of crumb mixture into a 9-inch pie pan. Layer half of oysters on top, then half of remaining crumbs, and remaining oysters. In a small bowl, combine oyster liquor, half and half, sherry and Worcestershire sauce. Pour over oysters in pan. Sprinkle with remaining crumbs. Bake 30 minutes or until top is golden. Serve hot, plain or with a chili sauce. Makes 3 to 4 servings.

Hangtown Fry

Hangtown, California where this dish originated, was a mining town. The dish consists of fried oysters and scrambled eggs. When the scrambled eggs are piled into a prebaked pie shell and the fried oysters laid on top, it becomes a "Hangtown Pie."

    4 bacon slices
    1 pint (about 24) fresh shucked oysters
    1 egg, beaten
    1/2 cup dry bread crumbs
    4 eggs
    2 tablespoons milk

In a medium-sized skillet, cook bacon until crisp. Remove to a warm plate. Dip oysters in beaten egg, then in bread crumbs. Fry on both sides in hot bacon drippings until golden. In a small bowl, beat 4 eggs and milk together. Add to oysters in skillet. Gently stir egg mixture around oysters without disturbing them. Turn mixture out of skillet omelet-style and top with crisp bacon. Makes 4 servings.

Baked Scallops with Crumbs & Cheese

Scallops are a sweet-tasting, mild shellfish. In Europe, they're fished along the Atlantic coasts and come with the coral attached. American scallops range from the tiny bay scallops to very large varieties, and are usually not sold in the shell or with the coral. New England has a profusion of scallop dishes, of which this simple one is the most basic.

    1 pint scallops
    10 butter crackers, crushed
    2 eggs, beaten
    1/2 cup butter, cut into pieces
    Grated Parmesan cheese (optional)

Preheat oven to 350F (175C). Grease 4 shallow, individual, baking dishes. Roll each scallop in cracker crumbs, then dip in beaten egg and roll in cracker crumbs again. Place in 4 greased baking dishes in a single layer. Top each with pieces of butter and sprinkle with Parmesan cheese, if desired. Bake 25 minutes or until tops are golden. Makes 4 servings.

Crab Cakes

— ◆ —

Crabs along with lobsters, shrimp and a host of other shellfish were fished along the coastal waters from New England southward. Crab cakes have been a favorite in Southern cooking since early Colonial days.

1 pound fresh or thawed, frozen crabmeat
2 tablespoons unsalted butter
1/2 cup *each* chopped onions, chopped celery, chopped green
bell pepper
2 garlic cloves, minced or pressed
1/4 cup all-purpose flour
1/2 cup whipping cream or milk
3 eggs, beaten
1 tablespoon chopped fresh parsley
1 teaspoon Worcestershire sauce
2 cups soft bread crumbs
1/2 teaspoon freshly ground black pepper
1 cup soft bread crumbs
Vegetable oil

Pick out and discard any shell or cartilage from crabmeat. In a large heavy skillet, heat butter. Add onions, celery, green pepper and garlic. Sauté over low heat about 5 minutes or until soft. Stir in flour. Add cream or milk. Cook, stirring, until thickened. Remove from heat; pour into a medium-sized bowl. Blend in eggs, crabmeat, parsley, Worcestershire sauce, 2 cups bread crumbs, salt and pepper. Refrigerate mixture until stiff. Shape into 12 equal-size cakes. Press 1 cup bread crumbs onto both sides of cakes. In a large heavy skillet, heat 1/4 inch vegetable oil over medium heat. Add crab cakes, a few at a time. Cook 3 to 4 minutes on each side or until browned. Remove to a warm platter. Serve immediately. Makes 6 servings.

✦ GRAINS, BEANS & PASTA ✦

Each ethnic group that settled in America contributed a "favorite starch" to our cuisine. The Scandinavians, English and other Northern Europeans preferred potatoes and you will find favorite recipes included in the Vegetables & Side Dishes section of this book, page 105. The Spanish, French, Greeks and Italians were among those who contributed rice.

Rice was first cultivated in America in the 1600s but every tale and legend credits a different person with the first crop. It was originally grown in South Carolina which to this day is a leading producer of rice.

In the early days of American life, beans of many varieties provided a storage-stable food which was high in vegetable protein. Combined with rice, beans provide a complete protein and dishes such as Hopping John and Red Beans & Rice are exemplary Southern classics.

Corn which is indigenous to our country, was cultivated by Native Americans and was quickly adopted by early settlers. When ground into meal it became a staple ingredient for American cooks. "Hoe cakes" which were pancakes purportedly baked on a hoe over an open fire, corn breads and puddings form the simplest and most basic products of early American cookery. Most of them are created by varying the proportion of cornmeal to liquid. Italians who quickly recognized the similarity between cornmeal and the food of the wealthy in northern Italy "puls," made polenta with the cornmeal. They sent the corn seed back to northern Italy where cornmeal remains today a staple of the Italian diet.

It was the Italians, 4 million of them arriving between 1820 and 1920 and hired to build railroads, who resisted the beans and potatoes offered as standard fare. As a result spaghetti, lasagna and ravioli became American food!

Hopping John

---◆---

Beans and rice make a complete protein and the combination is used in a number of different Southern states. Some people prefer black-eyed peas and others red beans. Superstition has it that this dish was to be eaten on New Year's Day in order to have good fortune for the coming year. The name, according to one account, is said to have come from the custom of having little boys hop around the table before sitting down to eat. Considering the energy level of little boys, it probably wasn't a bad idea!

A variation, Red Beans & Rice, is also a popular Southern main dish. It may be cooked with a ham hock instead of bacon.

To complete either menu, serve with a green salad and freshly baked biscuits or bread.

> 1 cup dried black-eyed peas or 2 cups shelled, fresh,
>   black-eyed peas
> 4 thick bacon slices, cut into 1/2-inch pieces
> 1 cup chopped onion
> 1 cup chopped green bell pepper
> 1 garlic clove, minced
> About 2 cups water
> 1 teaspoon salt
> 1 bay leaf
> 1/16 teaspoon red (cayenne) pepper
> 3 cups cooked long-grain rice

Wash beans and pick over, removing any pebbles or dirt. Add cold water to cover. Soak 12 hours or overnight. The quick-soak method can be used, page 14. If using fresh peas, this is not necessary. Rinse peas and drain. Cook bacon in a Dutch oven until browned. Add onion, green pepper and garlic. Sauté until onion is tender. Add beans or peas, 2 cups water and seasonings. Cover and simmer 40 to 50 minutes or until beans or peas are tender, adding water as necessary. Remove bay leaf. Stir in cooked rice. Cover and continue simmering about 10 minutes or until liquid is absorbed. Makes 6 servings.

Variation
Red Beans & Rice: Soak red beans as directed in Hopping John, above. Drain beans and place in a large pot. If desired, add 1 (1-pound) smoked ham hock. Add cold water to cover. Omit bacon and green pepper. Add onion, garlic, salt, bay leaf and red pepper. Bring to a boil, then reduce heat and simmer, covered, about 3 hours or until beans are tender. Serve over hot cooked rice. Makes about 6 servings.

Wild Rice & Pecan Dressing

— ◆ —

Pecans are the nuts of a tall hickory tree which is native to North America. Pecans are second to peanuts in popularity and besides being used in pies, candies and confections, make a wonderful flavor combination with wild rice. The Algonquin Indian word "paccan" or the Cree Indian word "pakan" are believed to be the origin of the name for the nut.

2/3 cup uncooked wild rice
2-1/2 cups water
6 tablespoons butter
1 large onion, thinly sliced
1 cup coarsely chopped pecans
1 slice whole-wheat bread, crumbled
2 ounces turkey ham
1 garlic clove, minced
1 teaspoon salt
1/4 teaspoon freshly ground black pepper
1/4 cup fresh parsley, packed into a cup

Wash wild rice in 3 changes of hot tap water. Place in a medium-sized saucepan with water. Simmer, covered, 45 minutes or until water is absorbed. In a large skillet, heat butter. Add onion and pecans. Sauté over low heat 20 minutes or until pecans are toasted and onion is soft. Preheat oven to 400F (205C). Meanwhile, combine bread, turkey ham, garlic, salt, pepper and parsley in a food processor fitted with the steel blade. Process until finely minced. Add onion and pecans; process using on/off pulses until coarsely chopped. Turn into a medium-sized bowl. Fold in cooked wild rice. Turn into a 1-1/2-quart casserole. Bake, covered, 30 minutes. Makes 6 servings.

Cajun Dirty Rice

Despite the unattractive name, which by the way is classic, this is a favorite, economical, main dish in the South. The method is the same as for Pilaf, page 66, with meats and vegetables being cooked with onion as the first step.

6 chicken gizzards
Water
1/2 cup chicken fat or vegetable oil
2 chicken livers
1/2 pound ground beef
1 large onion, chopped
1 green bell pepper, chopped
3 celery stalks, chopped
2 garlic cloves, minced or pressed
1/4 teaspoon red (cayenne) pepper
1 to 2 teaspoons salt
2 bay leaves
1/2 teaspoon dried leaf thyme
2 cups water
2 cups uncooked long-grain rice
4 green onions, chopped
1/4 cup chopped fresh parsley

Place gizzards in a medium-sized saucepan. Add water to barely cover. Bring to a boil; reduce heat and simmer about 30 minutes or until gizzards are tender. Set aside with cooking liquid. In a Dutch oven or other heavy pot, heat chicken fat or oil. Add chicken livers. Sauté 10 minutes or until livers are cooked through. Remove livers; set aside. Add ground beef and onion to pot with oil. Cook, breaking meat apart until no longer pink. Add green pepper and celery. Cook 10 minutes or until vegetables are tender but not brown. Put chicken livers and gizzards with cooking liquid into a blender or food processor fitted with the steel blade. Process until finely chopped. Add to beef mixture with garlic, red pepper, salt, bay leaves, thyme and 2 cups water. Stir in rice. Simmer, uncovered, 30 minutes or until rice is tender and liquid is absorbed. Remove bay leaves. Add chopped green onions and parsley. Let stand 10 minutes before serving. Makes about 6 main-dish servings.

Pilaf

—— • ◆ • ——

Pilaf, a blend of rice with chicken, shrimp or other ingredients is a popular Southern dish. Each locality has its own version. The pronunciation varies from Charleston to New Orleans from pilau or pilaf, pronounced with the "f," to "perloo" or "perlowe". The dish is of Persian or Turkish origin but was known in England as far back as 1612. Pilaf is most common in regions where French and Spanish cookery abound. In the South, "Dirty Rice", page 65, a variation of pilaf, is a favorite main dish. Still another variation of pilaf, Limping Susan, is a combination of rice, bacon, okra, salt and pepper.

> **2 tablespoons butter**
> **1 small onion, chopped**
> **1 cup uncooked long-grain rice**
> **2 cups chicken, beef, clam or vegetable broth**
> **1/2 teaspoon salt**
> **1/2 teaspoon paprika (optional)**
> **1/4 cup chopped fresh parsley**

In a 2-quart saucepan, heat butter. Add onion. Cook over medium heat about 5 minutes or until onion is translucent. Add rice. Stir until golden, about 5 minutes. Add broth, salt and paprika, if desired. Cover and bring to a boil. Reduce heat and simmer 20 to 25 minutes or until all liquid has been absorbed. Fluff rice with a fork; mix in chopped parsley. Makes 4 to 6 servings.

Souffléed Grits

The Indians taught the early settlers how to prepare hominy which turned out to be an important basic food. It was and still is made with yellow dent corn or the standard field corn which when dried has a "dent" in the top of each kernel. According to the old method, the corn was dried on the plant. When it was completely dry, it was picked and stored for processing later in the fall. Early settlers used lye made from wood ashes to treat the hominy. The dried corn was soaked in water with the lye until the grains puffed up to triple or quadruple their original size. The corn was then boiled for 2 hours or until the hulls slipped off. Next, it went through several soakings with fresh water after which it could be drained and frozen, or dried and ground into a meal.

To serve it plain and buttered, the hominy is soaked overnight in fresh water. Then it is boiled until all the water has evaporated, buttered while hot and served in place of potatoes. Ground hominy is called *grits* and has a texture slightly coarser than cornmeal.

> 5 cups water
> 1 cup hominy grits
> 2 eggs, separated
> 1/2 cup whipping cream
> 1 teaspoon salt
> 1/4 teaspoon white pepper

Boil water in a medium-sized saucepan. Stir in grits. Cook over low heat 25 to 30 minutes, stirring occasionally. Cool. Preheat oven to 350F (175C). Grease a 1-quart casserole. Blend yolks into cooked grits. Add cream, salt and pepper. In a medium-sized bowl, beat egg whites until they stand in peaks; fold into grits. Spoon into greased casserole. Bake 35 to 40 minutes or until puffed and golden. Serve immediately. Makes 4 servings.

Classic New England Baked Beans

———————————— ◆ ————————————

This is the most frequently copied of the New England foods. Western versions vary so much from the original that they defy first-sight recognition. Food historians note that the making of brown bread and baked beans were cooking skills first learned from the Indians. Puritans in the Boston area observed how nearby Indians cooked their earthen pots of beans in glowing coals mixed with ashes. At the time, the Puritans had a 24-hour cooking ban that started with the beginning of their Sabbath at sundown on Saturday. They set their filled bean pots at the sides of their fireplaces and kept them warm to cook and increase the flavor of their dish.

Serve with Boston Brown Bread, page 148, Coleslaw with Boiled Dressing, page 120, relishes and pickles of choice, and Apple Pie, page 188, to have the classic menu for church suppers and community gatherings.

> **1 pound pea beans, navy beans or great northern beans**
> **Water**
> **2 teaspoons salt**
> **1/2 teaspoon mustard powder**
> **1/4 cup molasses**
> **1-1/2 to 2 tablespoons brown sugar**
> **1/4 pound salt pork, rind scored**

Wash beans and pick over, removing any pebbles or dirt. Place in a large pot. Add cold water to cover. Soak overnight. Drain. Add fresh water to cover. Bring to a boil; boil about 1-1/2 hours or until bean skins begin to break but beans are intact. To test, remove a few beans with a spoon. Blow over them, skins should ruffle. The quick-soak method can be used, page 14. Turn beans with their liquid into an earthenware pot. Add salt, mustard, molasses and brown sugar. Press piece of salt pork, rind-side up, into center of beans so it is even with top of beans. Add enough water to not quite cover beans. Place in oven and set at 300F (150C). Bake, uncovered, just until beans begin to simmer, 45 minutes to 1 hour. Cover. Bake 8 hours, adding more boiling water occasionally as liquid evaporates. Remove lid for last 30 minutes so juices will boil down. Don't stir, this would mash up beans and they should remain whole. Makes 10 to 12 servings.

Variations
Connecticut-Style Beans: Bury a large peeled onion in beans before baking. Some cooks first stick onion with 4 or 5 whole cloves.
Cape Cod Beans: Pour 1/2 cup whipping cream over beans during last 30 minutes of baking.
Vermont-Style Beans: Substitute maple syrup for molasses and brown sugar.
Autumn-Style Beans: Bury a bay leaf in beans below salt pork. Add 4 cups fresh whole-kernel corn to beans during last 30 minutes of baking.

Frijoles

Pronounced "free-ho-les," these are the buff-colored beans with brown spots, or pinto beans which are most often prepared by Southwestern cooks. Directions usually say to soak the beans overnight, but many experienced bean cooks don't. They start the beans in lukewarm water and add a bit of diced salt pork or bacon rinds and scraps and let them simmer 2 hours. The beans are usually seasoned with garlic and red chili, then mashed and pan-fried. Commonly called *refried beans*, these can be spread on small, crisp tortillas and topped with cheese and shredded lettuce to make tostadas.

Macaroni & Cheese

— ◆ —

Macaroni, along with pasta in general is an enormously important Italian contribution to American cooking. Macaroni, shaped in long sticks, could have been the first pasta to be in general use among Americans of all ethnic backgrounds. Several recipes appear in an 1879 edition of *Housekeeping in Old Virginia* by Tyre. President Jefferson, who entertained frequently and set culinary standards which have never been matched in the White House, served "a pie called macaroni" at a dinner in February 1802 according to a visiting preacher, Mr. Manasseh Cutler.

> **2-1/2 cups elbow macaroni, or long macaroni, broken into**
>   **1-inch pieces**
> **1 small onion, peeled**
> **1/4 cup butter**
> **1/4 cup all-purpose flour**
> **2-1/4 cups milk**
> **1 teaspoon mustard powder**
> **1 teaspoon salt**
> **Dash of freshly ground black pepper**
> **2 eggs**
> **2 cups (8 ounces) shredded Cheddar cheese**
> **1/2 cup dry bread crumbs**
> **Butter**

Cook macaroni in boiling water with 1 onion added, until macaroni is tender but firm to the bite. Drain macaroni; discard onion. Preheat oven to 400F (205C). While macaroni cooks, heat butter in a small saucepan. Stir in flour and cook 1 minute. Add milk, a little at a time. Cook, stirring, until sauce thickens and bubbles. Add mustard, salt and pepper. In a small bowl, whisk eggs. Add a small amount of sauce to eggs, then mix egg mixture into sauce. Set aside about 1/4 cup cheese for top. In a 2-quart baking dish or casserole, arrange alternate layers of macaroni and cheese. Pour sauce over all; sprinkle with reserved cheese, bread crumbs and some small pieces of butter. Bake 35 minutes or until top is browned. Makes 4 to 6 servings.

Spatzle

─────────────── •◆• ───────────────

This cross between noodles and dumplings was brought to the United States by immigrants from Austria and Hungary.

2 cups all-purpose flour
2 teaspoons salt
1 tablespoon farina
2 eggs
Water
1/4 cup butter, melted

In a medium-sized bowl, combine flour, 1 teaspoon salt and farina. Blend in eggs and enough water to make a thick stiff dough. Bring a pot of water to a boil and add remaining salt to it. Turn dough onto a board. Cut into almond-sized pieces. Drop into boiling water to make dumplings. Or, press through a spatzle maker into boiling water. After dumplings rise, cook 1 to 2 minutes longer. Remove from water with a slotted spoon. Turn into a warm serving dish. Toss with melted butter. Makes 4 servings.

Benny's Mother's Filled Polenta

—◆—

I asked a second-generation American, Benny, what his Italian-born mother made for a quick meal when he was a kid. "Quick meal?" Benny shot back, "There was no such thing as a quick meal!" Digging further, I asked what his favorite food was. "Polenta!" he rolled his eyes and looked heavenward, "Ahh, the polenta . . .with mozzarella, with fried peppers, with garlic . . ."

This is a "filled polenta." The vegetable filling can be varied as desired, and you can also adjust the amount of cheese.

Filling, see below
Polenta, see below
2 tablespoons freshly grated Parmesan cheese
1/2 cup (2 ounces) shredded mozzarella cheese

Filling:
1 red bell pepper
2 tablespoons olive oil
1 small red onion, chopped
1 garlic clove, minced or pressed
3 tomatoes, peeled, seeded, diced (1-1/2 cups diced)
1/4 cup chopped fresh basil or 1 tablespoon dried leaf basil
1 teaspoon sugar
Salt and freshly ground black pepper to taste

Polenta:
1-1/2 cups cornmeal
5 cups water
1 teaspoon salt
2 tablespoons freshly grated Parmesan cheese
1/2 cup (2 ounces) shredded mozzarella cheese

Preheat oven to 450F (230C). Grease a shallow, 1-1/2-quart, baking dish. Prepare Filling; set aside. Prepare Polenta. Pour half of polenta mixture into greased dish. Top with half of filling, then remaining polenta. Top with remaining filling. Sprinkle with 2 table-spoons Parmesan and 1/2 cup mozzarella cheese. You can do this ahead; refrigerate. Before serving, bake 20 minutes or until cheese is melted and polenta is bubbly around edges. If refrigerated, it will take 5 to 10 minutes longer. Makes 6 servings.

To prepare Filling: Preheat broiler. Broil red pepper 3 inches from source of heat, turning, about 10 minutes or until evenly charred. Place in a paper bag; cool. Peel pepper; discard core and seeds. Chop pepper. In a large heavy skillet, heat olive oil over medium to low heat. Add onion and garlic. Sauté 3 minutes or until soft and aromatic. Add red pepper, tomatoes, basil, sugar, salt and black pepper. Simmer 3 minutes longer or until watery liquid has evaporated. Remove from heat; set aside.

To prepare Polenta: In a medium-sized bowl, mix cornmeal and 1 cup cold water. In a large saucepan, bring remaining 4 cups water with 1 teaspoon salt to a boil. Slowly whisk in cornmeal and cook, whisking constantly, 20 minutes or until thick and smooth. Remove from heat; stir in 2 tablespoons Parmesan and 1/2 cup mozzarella cheese.

Cheddar Cornmeal Loaf

———————————————— •◆• ————————————————

This is a variation of Hasty Pudding which was a loaf of cooked cornmeal, chilled and cut into slices, dipped in batter and fried in hot butter or bacon fat until crisp and golden. It was served with maple syrup. This version is mixed with Cheddar cheese, another classic American product. The fried slices are served for breakfast or lunch with ham, sausages or crisp bacon.

> **1 cup cornmeal**
> **1 cup milk**
> **2 cups boiling water**
> **1 teaspoon salt**
> **1/2 pound medium to sharp Cheddar cheese, cubed**
> **Flour**
> **1/2 cup butter, bacon fat or vegetable shortening**

Lightly grease a 9″ x 5″ loaf pan. In a large heavy saucepan, combine cornmeal and milk. Add boiling water and cook, stirring, over medium heat until thick. Reduce to low and cook, covered, 10 minutes, stirring occasionally. Remove from heat. Add salt and cheese, stirring until cheese melts. Spoon into greased loaf pan. Cool until solid. Turn out of pan and cut into slices about 3/4 inch thick. Dust slices lightly with flour. In a large heavy skillet, heat fat. Fry slices in hot fat until crisp and golden on both sides. Makes 4 to 6 servings.

✦ HEARTY SOUPS & STEWS ✦

A cauldron of soup hanging over an open hearth paints a classic scene in the early American kitchen. Old cookbooks credit all kinds of psychological and physical advantages to soup. It was variously prescribed as a remedy for the hungry, the fat, the tired, the worried, those in pain, in debt or in love. Not to mention that "useless" pieces of meat or poultry (in that they are old and tough) can be simmered to tenderness when making soup.

Each ethnic group has added to the American repertoire. The Scandinavians gave us potato soups and pea soups, the English added chowders, the Italians contributed wonderful vegetable, fish and pasta soups just to mention a few.

But as Americans, we aren't inclined to keep anything the same. The soups meld. Creole gumbo is a classic example. This soup-stew, blends classic French cuisine with that of the Spanish and Anglo-Saxons. It uses herbs and spices from both France and Spain and the cooking techniques learned from the Choctaw and Chicasaw Indians. All this is blended with the exotic taste and seasoning abilities of African cooks. Creole cookery is born of these ingredients combined with the ingenuity of refugee Acadians (Cajuns) who had to learn the use of nature's own foods wherever they were.

The Pennsylvania Dutch blend German and middle-European cookery with available ingredients to make sturdy soups that are meals in themselves. They have a basic simplicity. The simplest of soups are milk-based and are recorded in early Pennsylvania Dutch recipes. One called *pretzel soup* was simply dried pretzels broken into a bowl, dotted with butter and hot milk poured over. Another, called *poor man's soup* is hot milk with spatzle noodles added.

There are soups that have historical significance. The citizens of Plymouth ate a special succotash soup on December 21st, Forefather's Day. With it they served hot Johnnycake and Indian Pudding. The meal was to commemorate the landing of the Pilgrims.

New England Clam Chowder

It is natural that the native food of the Northeast should be fish. This is the home of the "bean and the cod," where the fishing industry is vitally important. "Shore Dinners" that started with clam chowder and included steamed clams, boiled lobster and corn on the cob are traditional with Yankee cooks. But these menus were started by the Indians who made periodical treks to the seashore to feast on seafood.

Typical of the disagreements that surround regional foods, is the ongoing controversy about tomatoes in clam chowder. Cooks in Rhode Island and Connecticut like to include tomato, although we generally think of it as Manhattan clam chowder. The other four New England states are united against this "culinary crime," and the Maine legislature once introduced a bill to outlaw the mixing of clams and tomatoes! Rhode Island cooks use quahogs, the Indian name for hard-shell clams in their chowder, while Massachusetts chooses soft-shell clams. All chowders start with salt pork and include onions, potatoes and clams. Most include milk, although some in Connecticut use water, and of course, some use tomatoes. Most native cooks ladle the hot chowder over split common crackers. These are crackers that are thick and flaky, known as *Boston* or *pilot crackers*.

> 1/4 pound salt pork, rind removed, pork cut into 1/2-inch dice
> 1 large onion, cut into 1/2-inch dice
> 2 large potatoes, cut into 1/2-inch dice
> Water
> 1 pint fresh shucked clams in liquor
> 1-1/2 cups half and half or 1 (12-ounce) can evaporated milk,
>   undiluted
> 1 teaspoon salt
> 1/4 teaspoon freshly ground black pepper
> 1 tablespoon butter
> Additional whole milk
> Common crackers or soda crackers

In a medium-sized heavy skillet, cook salt pork until crisp. Meanwhile, in a medium-sized saucepan, simmer onion and potatoes in water to cover 10 minutes. Add clams and cook 10 minutes longer. Add salt pork. Reduce heat to low. Add half and half or evaporated milk, salt, pepper, butter and additional whole milk, as desired. Heat through; do not boil. Serve over split crackers. Makes 4 servings.

Note: The word "chowder" is thought to be derived from the French copper pot "la chaudière." An old French custom was to greet a homecoming fisherman with a feast cooked in the pot. The tradition carried over to the eastern Canadian and New England coast where "la chaudière" became "chowder."

Manhattan Clam Chowder

◆

This is the chowder that is made with tomatoes, an unthinkable ingredient to die-hard New Englanders!

    1/2 pound bacon slices, chopped
    4 medium-sized onions, chopped
    4 carrots, chopped
    2 celery stalks, chopped
    2 tablespoons chopped fresh parsley
    1 (28-ounce) can tomatoes
    1 pint fresh shucked clams in liquor
    Water
    1-1/2 teaspoons dried leaf thyme
    1 bay leaf
    3 medium-sized potatoes, diced
    Salt and freshly ground black pepper to taste

In a large soup pot, cook bacon until crisp. Drain off all but 2 tablespoons bacon drippings. Add onions, carrots, celery and parsley. Cook on low to medium heat 8 minutes or until vegetables are soft. Drain tomatoes and clams, reserving liquid. Add clam liquor to tomato liquid and enough water to equal 6 cups. Add to pot with vegetables and thyme, bay leaf and potatoes. Simmer, covered, 40 minutes. Add clams, tomatoes, salt and pepper. Heat to serving temperature. Makes 6 servings.

Oyster Stew

◆

Oysters along with soft- and hard-shelled clams, scallops, mussels and other shellfish, giant crabs and lobsters were part of the native bounty the early settlers found in America. Oysters are important all along the Atlantic coastline to New Orleans.

This stew appears on Christmas Eve and was also traditionally served at New England community Watch-Party services on New Year's Eve. On one rule all agree, that the stew is not to be thickened. Milk, cream or half and half is the only liquid.

    1 pint fresh shucked oysters in liquor
    1/4 cup butter
    1 cup half and half
    3 cups milk
    Freshly ground black pepper to taste
    1/2 teaspoon salt
    1/2 teaspoon paprika

Put oysters and butter into a medium-sized heavy saucepan and heat slowly until edges of oysters curl. Scald half and half and milk by heating almost to boiling point. Add hot half and half and milk to oysters. Return to boiling point; remove from heat. Add pepper, salt and paprika. Serve immediately with oyster crackers. Makes 4 servings.

New Orleans Filé Gumbo

—————————— • ♦ • ——————————

This is an interesting dish to serve as a main course for supper during the holiday season when oysters and other seafoods are more available. Vary the seafood as you wish or follow this recipe for a tasty gumbo.

Filé is a powder made from the tender young leaves of sassafras. It is used as a flavoring and thickener. Choctaw Indian squaws used to bring filé into the French market in New Orleans to sell. Today it can be found in gourmet spice shops. This is an elegant and expensive recipe for most of us but on the Gulf Coast it was a matter of using the most readily available ingredients!

> 1 tablespoon butter
> 1 medium-sized onion, chopped
> 1 teaspoon minced fresh parsley
> 1 tablespoon all-purpose flour
> 1 quart oyster liquor
> 1 pint boiling water
> Salt and freshly ground black pepper to taste
> 1 bay leaf
> 1 cup peeled cooked shrimp
> 1 cup crabmeat
> 12 fresh oysters, shucked
> 1 cooked chicken breast, diced
> 1 tablespoon filé powder
> Hot cooked rice

In a large heavy skillet, heat butter. Add onion. Sauté until lightly browned. Add parsley and flour. Gradually add oyster liquor, boiling water, salt, pepper and bay leaf, stirring constantly until blended and boiling. Add seafood and chicken; stir gently. Cook only until edges of oysters curl. Remove from heat. Carefully sift or sprinkle in filé, stirring gently to prevent filé from lumping. Do not reheat once filé has been added. Turn into a warmed tureen. Serve in soup bowls over hot cooked rice. Makes 6 to 8 servings.

Texas Shrimp Gumbo

— ◆ —

Although we often think of Texas as a beef state, it does border Louisiana and a large part of it lies along the Gulf of Mexico. This gumbo is considered a Texan classic.

> 4 quarts water
> 1/4 cup shrimp or crab boil
> 2-1/2 pounds shrimp, peeled, deveined
> 3 tablespoons butter
> 3 tablespoons bacon drippings
> 1 cup *each* diced celery, onion and green green pepper
> 1 (28-ounce) can tomatoes
> 1 teaspoon dried leaf thyme
> 1 garlic clove, minced
> 1 bay leaf
> 1 teaspoon Worcestershire sauce
> 1 tablespoon filé powder
> 1 teaspoon salt
> 1/2 teaspoon freshly ground black pepper
> 1 (10-ounce) package thawed, frozen, cut okra
> 1/4 cup uncooked long-grain rice

In a large pot, bring water to a boil. Tie shrimp or crab boil in a cheesecloth bag. Add to water with shrimp. Bring to a boil. Reduce heat and simmer 10 minutes. Turn off heat; let stand 10 minutes. Drain shrimp, reserving 2 cups broth. In a heavy Dutch oven, heat butter and bacon drippings. Add celery, onion and green pepper. Cook until tender. Add shrimp broth, tomatoes with juice, thyme, garlic, bay leaf, Worcestershire sauce, filé powder, salt and pepper to vegetable mixture. Simmer, covered, 45 minutes. Add okra and rice. Simmer, covered, 30 minutes or until rice is tender. Add shrimp and heat through. Makes 8 servings.

Scandinavian Potato & Salmon Chowder

— ◆ —

Poached fish left from an earlier meal is perfect to use in this soup. Besides salmon you could use any firm-fleshed fish such as cod, trout, whitefish or haddock.

1 pint milk (2 cups)
1 large potato, pared, diced
1/3 cup diced celery
1 small onion, minced
3/4 cup water
2 tablespoons butter
2 tablespoons all-purpose flour
1 (15-ounce) can pink or red salmon, skin and bones removed
1 tablespoon tomato paste
Salt and freshly ground black pepper to taste

Scald milk by heating almost to boiling point. Put potato, celery and onion into a large saucepan. Add water to barely cover vegetables. Simmer about 10 minutes until soft but not mushy. In a medium-sized pan, heat butter. Add flour and stir until blended. Gradually stir in hot milk, whisking until smooth and thickened. Add to vegetables with salmon, can juices and tomato paste. Taste and add salt and pepper if needed. Makes 4 generous servings.

Cheddar-Cheese Soup

—◆—

As America is a melting pot of cuisines, so cheese melts into the soup pot, too. The idea of a cheese soup is one that comes from many cuisines. An Italian version is made with pepperoni and Parmesan cheese, another combines bourbon and Swiss cheese. Others use cream cheese and potatoes or Swiss cheese and shallots. An interesting goat's-cheese soup is heady with garlic and mustard sprouts. Cheddar-Cheese Soup to my mind is the most American and combines our own Cheddar cheese with vegetables.

2 tablespoons butter
1 small onion, minced
1 small carrot, shredded
1/4 cup finely chopped green bell pepper
1/4 cup finely chopped celery
3 tablespoons all-purpose flour
5 cups chicken broth
2 cups (8 ounces) shredded Cheddar cheese
1 to 1-1/2 cups milk
Salt to taste
White pepper or red (cayenne) pepper to taste

In a 3-quart saucepan, heat butter. Add onion, carrot, green pepper and celery. Sauté 6 to 8 minutes or until soft but not browned. Turn vegetables into a blender or food processor fitted with the steel blade. While processing, add flour and broth. Return to saucepan and bring to a boil, whisking constantly until soup thickens. Reduce heat and simmer, partially covered, about 10 minutes. Whisk in cheese, a handful at a time. Cook until cheese dissolves, then pour in 1 cup milk, adding 1/2 cup more if soup is too thick. Taste for seasoning and add salt and white and red pepper. Heat to serving temperature. Soup is good either hot or cold. Makes 6 to 8 servings.

Variation
Milwaukee Beer-Cheese Soup: Substitute 1 (12-ounce) can or bottle dark beer for milk. Add 1 cup whipping cream to soup before serving.

Wild-Rice & Mushroom Soup

— ◆ —

Native Americans of northern Minnesota use wild rice as a staple in their diet. The rice is actually not rice at all but the seed of a grass which grows in the water-flooded paddies of northern lakes. It is probably more closely related to barley than to rice. Settlers in these northern parts soon learned to appreciate the heady flavor and nourishment of this natural grain. Recipes for wild-rice and mushroom soup are among the most popular. The soup is especially good when made with fresh wild mushrooms which can be found in wooded areas.

Northern Indians have traditionally cooked wild rice in fat, and in so doing, created a kind of "popped rice." It does not actually "pop" in the fat but expands to three times its original size. These crispy morsels make great appetizers simply sprinkled with a bit of seasoning or eaten plain. They can also be used to garnish soup.

Popped Wild Rice, see below
1/2 cup uncooked wild rice
1-1/2 cups water
3 tablespoons butter
2 green onions, thinly sliced, including tops
1/2 pound fresh mushrooms, sliced
1/4 cup all-purpose flour
1 quart chicken broth
1/2 pint whipping cream or half and half (1 cup)
2 tablespoons dry sherry

Popped Wild Rice:
Vegetable oil
Wild rice

Prepare Popped Wild Rice; set aside. Wash 1/2 cup wild rice in 3 changes of hot tap water. Add to 1-1/2 cups water in a medium-sized saucepan. Bring to a boil. Reduce heat and simmer, covered, 35 to 45 minutes or until rice is tender. In a medium-sized saucepan, heat butter. Add green onions and mushrooms. Sauté 3 to 5 minutes or until onions are transparent. Add flour and cook, stirring, 2 minutes. Stir in chicken broth. Bring to a boil, stirring until thickened. Add boiled wild rice, cream or half and half and sherry, stirring until heated through. Garnish with Popped Wild Rice. Makes 6 servings.
To prepare Popped Wild Rice: Pour oil 1/2 inch deep in a large heavy skillet. Place a wire strainer in oil as you heat oil almost to smoking point. Add 1 tablespoon wild rice to oil in strainer. Remove with strainer as soon as wild rice stops popping. Drain on paper towels. Repeat. One tablespoon unpopped wild rice gives about 3 tablespoons popped.

Country Garden-Vegetable Soup

—◆—

Use fresh garden vegetables or substitute an equivalent amount of frozen or canned, preferably home-processed vegetables.

> 1 large soup bone with meat
> 1 pound lean beef stew meat, cut into 2-inch cubes
> 2 tablespoons vegetable oil
> 2 quarts water
> 1 bay leaf
> 4 whole black peppercorns
> 1/3 cup pearl barley
> 1 medium-sized onion, chopped
> 2 cups mixed sliced carrots, chopped celery, whole-kernel corn
>   and fresh or frozen green peas
> 1 quart chopped fresh tomatoes, or 1 quart home-canned
>   tomatoes, or 2 (16-ounce) cans whole or stewed tomatoes
> 3 parsley sprigs, chopped
> 1/4 teaspoon *each* dried leaf rosemary, marjoram and thyme
> Salt and freshly ground black pepper to taste

In a large, heavy, soup pot, brown soup bone and stew meat in oil over medium to high heat, slowly turning meat to brown on all sides. Remove from heat and carefully add water, bay leaf and peppercorns. Reduce heat and simmer, covered, 1-1/2 to 2 hours. Remove bone. Skim fat from top of broth. Add barley; simmer 45 minutes. Add onion, carrots, celery, corn, peas, tomatoes and herbs. Simmer, covered, 25 minutes or until vegetables are tender. Remove bay leaf. Add salt and pepper. Makes 10 to 12 servings.

Maine Corn Chowder

—•◆•—

Warming bowls of hot soup and a loaf of fresh-baked bread makes up the menu of many country suppers. This is quick to make with ingredients that can be easily kept on hand.

> 1 large onion, chopped
> 3 large potatoes, diced
> Water
> 1 (16-ounce) can cream-style corn
> 1-1/2 cups evaporated milk or 1 (12-ounce) can, undiluted
> 2 tablespoons butter
> Salt and freshly ground black pepper to taste

In a medium-sized saucepan, cook onion and potatoes in water to cover until vegetables are soft but not mushy. Add corn and evaporated milk. Heat through. Stir in butter, salt and pepper. Makes 4 generous servings.

Old-Fashioned Cream-of-Tomato Soup

—•◆•—

In season, there's nothing like a creamy tomato soup made from fresh tomatoes! In season, also, if you have enough tomatoes to make a pot of soup, country cooks often have enough tomatoes to can for wintertime enjoyment. One of my favorite ways to use home-canned tomatoes is in this simple, creamy soup.

> 2 tablespoons butter
> 1 small onion, finely chopped
> 1/4 cup all-purpose flour
> 1 cup milk
> 1 quart peeled, chopped, fresh tomatoes, or 1 quart
>   home-canned tomatoes, or 1 (28-ounce) can Italian-style
>   tomatoes
> 1/2 teaspoon dried leaf thyme
> 1/2 teaspoon dried leaf basil
> Salt and freshly ground black pepper to taste
> 1/2 pint whipping cream (1 cup)
> Celery leaf

In a large saucepan, heat butter. Add onion. Sauté 2 minutes. Add flour and cook, stirring, 2 minutes. Whisk in milk. Cook, stirring, until thickened. Add tomatoes with juice. Simmer 10 minutes. Turn mixture into a blender or food processor fitted with the steel blade. Process until fairly smooth. Return soup to pan. Add thyme, basil, salt and pepper. Stir in cream. Heat to serving temperature. Serve hot garnished with a celery leaf. Makes 4 to 6 servings.

Variation
Yellow-Tomato Soup: Substitute yellow tomatoes for red tomatoes.

Pennsylvania Dutch Chicken Rivvel Soup

⸻ • ♦ • ⸻

"The poor must eat what they have," was a saying of the early Pennsylvania settlers. Soup was an all-purpose food. "You don't have to have teeth to eat soup," was another popular adage. Soup was often all there was to eat and soup could be made out of just a very few ingredients. It was frugal and filling. Even if there was nothing but milk and flour in the cupboard, they could make two kinds of soup—brown-flour soup and rivvel soup. Presumably the availability of eggs was a given because it just required a trip to the henhouse to find one or two. Milk, potatoes and onions would make two more kinds of soup—potato soup and onion soup. Even after the days of extreme poverty, people continued to make these soups because they liked them. This one was made with old hens that were already quite tough and required a long, slow simmer to make them "eatable." Unless you have a chicken farm, it is difficult to get such tough, old hens today. However, a good soup can be made with a large stewing hen. The preroasting develops the chicken flavor.

1 (4- to 5-pound) stewing hen
1 large onion, finely chopped
1-1/2 teaspoons salt
1 teaspoon freshly ground black pepper
1 teaspoon dried leaf thyme
1/8 teaspoon ground mace
2 to 3 parsley sprigs
Water
Rivvels, see below
Minced fresh parsley
Crumbled cooked bacon
Chopped hard-cooked egg
2 tablespoons melted butter

Rivvels:
2 eggs
1-1/4 cups all-purpose flour
1/2 teaspoon salt
1/8 teaspoon freshly ground black pepper

Preheat oven to 400F (205C). Wash hen and pat dry with paper towels. Roast on a rack 45 minutes or until skin is golden and crackled. Place in a 5- to 6-quart soup pot. Add onion, salt, pepper, thyme, mace, parsley sprigs and water to cover. Bring to a boil. Reduce heat and simmer, partially covered, 45 minutes to 1 hour or until meat is very tender. Remove hen from pot. Remove and discard skin and bones. Pull meat into large shreds. Return meat to pot. Discard parsley. Skim off fat. Simmer soup over low heat. Prepare Rivels. Pick up a portion of Rivvel mixture at a time and pinch off pieces about the size of small marbles; drop into soup. Simmer 3 minutes or until Rivvels rise to surface. Taste and adjust seasonings, if necessary. To serve, sprinkle soup with minced parsley, bacon and hard-cooked egg; drizzle with butter. Makes about 8 servings.
To prepare Rivvels: Beat eggs in a medium-sized bowl using a whisk or a fork. Blend in flour, salt and pepper until mixture is moistened but still looks lumpy; do not overmix.

Country Pumpkin Soup

Native Americans Indians were excellent farmers and cultivated a dozen types of corn, beans, squashes and pumpkins which they introduced to the settlers. The farming success of the Indians may or may not have depended on some of their superstitions such as the one about the naked squaw. They believed that if she walked in the garden under a bright moon while dragging her clothes behind her, it would keep cutworms from destroying the vegetables.

> **1 pound diced, peeled, seeded pumpkin or butternut squash**
> **2 cups water**
> **1/2 teaspoon salt**
> **1/2 teaspoon sugar**
> **2/3 cup *each* cooking broth, orange juice and whipping cream**
> **2 teaspoons curry powder**

Put squash, water, salt and sugar into a large heavy saucepan. Simmer, covered, 15 minutes or until squash is cooked. Drain and turn into a blender or food processor fitted with the steel blade. Add cooking broth, orange juice, whipping cream and curry powder. Process until silky smooth. Return to pot and reheat or refrigerate and serve cold. Makes 4 servings.

Stacked Chicken Stew

This is an old recipe from Maine. The ingredients are "stacked" by being packed close together in a stew pot. Originally, the stew was simmered on top of the range but it is much less likely to burn on the bottom if it is baked in a slow oven.

1 (3-1/2-pound) chicken, cut up
4 potatoes, sliced
2 onions, sliced
Water
2 tablespoons butter
Salt and freshly ground black pepper to taste
12 saltine crackers, coarsely crumbled
1 cup half and half or whole milk
Minced fresh parsley

Preheat oven to 300F (150C). Remove fat and skin from chicken. Wash chicken and pat dry with paper towels. Layer chicken, potatoes and onions in a heavy Dutch oven. Add water to cover. Bake, covered, 1-1/2 hours or until tender. Cut butter into pieces; sprinkle over stew. Sprinkle with salt and pepper. Moisten crackers with half and half or milk; add crackers and remaining half and half or milk to stew. Cover and return to oven. Reheat to serving temperature. Sprinkle with parsley. Makes 8 servings.

Peanut Soup

This is a Southern classic that takes only minutes to prepare and looks festive topped with chopped peanuts.

3 cups chicken broth
1 cup peanut butter
1/8 teaspoon *each* celery salt, onion salt and sugar
1-1/2 cups whipping cream
Unsweetened whipped cream
Chopped peanuts

In a medium-sized saucepan, heat chicken broth to boiling. Add peanut butter, stirring until smooth. Season with celery salt, onion salt and sugar. Stir in whipping cream. Heat but do not boil. Top with unsweetened whipped cream and chopped peanuts. Makes 6 servings.

Old-Fashioned Split-Pea Soup with Ham

————————————————————— • ♦ • —————————————————————

Split peas are peas that have been dried until they split into two parts. Either yellow or green peas can be used in this soup.

> **2 cups split peas**
> **10 cups boiling water**
> **1 (12- to 16-ounce) ham hock**
> **1 large onion, chopped**
> **1 carrot, diced**
> **1/4 teaspoon freshly ground black pepper**
> **Salt to taste**

Wash and pick over peas. Place in a deep pot with boiling water. Add ham hock, onion, carrot and pepper. Simmer, covered, 1 to 1-1/2 hours or until peas are creamy and onions and carrots are very soft. Remove ham hock. Dice meat; discard bone. Return meat to pot. Skim off any excess fat. Taste and add salt, if necessary. Makes 8 servings.

Simple Oven Stew

————————————————————— • ♦ • —————————————————————

On small farms, the women often joined in with the men during haymaking and harvest chores. There wasn't much time for cooking, but appetites were keen. On the small farm where I grew up, this was a favorite "field-day stew" which could be left in the oven while we were all working outside.

> **2 pounds beef stew meat or lean beef chuck, cut into 2-inch**
> **   cubes**
> **2 medium-sized onions, quartered, sliced**
> **3 large carrots, sliced into 1/2-inch pieces**
> **1 teaspoon salt**
> **Dash of freshly ground black pepper**
> **1 pint whole tomatoes, preferably home-canned or 1 (16-ounce)**
> **   can, with juice**
> **3 large potatoes, quartered, cut into 1/2-inch slices**
> **1/4 cup all-purpose flour**

Combine all ingredients in a heavy 3-quart casserole with a tight-fitting lid. Place in oven. Set oven at 275F (135C). Bake 5 hours or until meat is done and vegetables are tender. At such a low heat, the vegetables steam to tenderness but do not become mushy. If juices are not thick, drain them from stew into a wide skillet. Bring to a boil; boil until reduced by half, then return juices to stew. Makes 6 to 8 servings.

Mulligan Stew or Mojakka

—◆—

I've always had the notion that "Mulligan" is a corrupted name for Irish stew. Irish stew, however, is made with lamb or mutton, and Mulligan with beef. Finnish Americans make a stew just like this which they call *Mojakka*, for some unknown reason. That word is not part of the Finnish language!

2 pounds beef stew meat, cut into 1-inch cubes
Cold water
4 medium-sized potatoes, quartered
4 medium-sized carrots, cut into 2-inch pieces
4 small onions, quartered
1 small (1/2-pound) rutabaga or turnip, cut into 1-inch dice
3 parsley sprigs
2 teaspoons salt
1/4 teaspoon freshly ground black pepper
1 tablespoon sugar
2 tablespoons all-purpose flour
1/2 cup water

Put meat into a 4-quart pot. Add cold water to cover. Bring to a boil. Add potatoes, carrots, onions, rutabaga or turnip, parsley, salt, pepper and sugar to boiling mixture. Simmer, tightly covered, over low heat 2-1/2 hours or until meat is tender. In a cup, blend flour and 1/2 cup water until smooth. Stir into boiling stew. Cook 15 minutes or until thickened, stirring frequently. Makes 8 servings.

─FINGER FOODS, SNACKS─ & SANDWICHES

Grandma might have called these *tidbits*, and in many country homes something as fancy sounding as "appetizer" was completely out of place. But there were occasions when company came and the table was laid with coffee, sweets and "something salty." In most old cookbooks, these tidbits were buried within the chapters on breads, meats or vegetables. Homemade sausages, cut into bits and fried, served on a hot plate with bowls of pickles or fresh vegetables, little meatballs, cheese sticks, and sandwiches are among the simplest and most satisfying snacks.

The cocktail party with its drinks and trays of hors d'oeuvres never quite made it into everyday country cooking. Entertaining never really was considered such because in the country, food was offered to everybody who happened to be around at mealtime.

There is little to distinguish between an appetizer and a snack. Grandma might offer tidbits today as she awaits the arrival of the entire party. Lunch that used to be "dinner," now might be finger food . . . sandwiches. And, dinner that used to be "supper," could be nothing but finger foods and snacks.

We've become adept at converting main dishes to finger-food-style service. A roast of beef, cooked rare, or a ham, thinly sliced, may be offered on a buffet next to little rye buns, mustards and other spreads for do-it-yourself sandwich-making. Meatballs might be served with wooden picks for spearing them along with vegetable dips and dunks. Remember that it takes some planning if one wants to be sure of offering a selection of informal food that will be somewhat "balanced." This consideration is as always, a vital ingredient in successful entertaining.

Hot Chili Con Queso

———— •◆• ————

This "hot chili with cheese" dip from the Mexican heritage of the American Southwest feeds right into our passion for dipping and dunking, munching and nibbling. Not searingly hot, but spicy and cheesy, this dip is good with fresh vegetables or corn chips.

> 2 tablespoons butter
> 1 small onion, finely minced (about 1/4 cup)
> 2 medium-sized tomatoes, peeled, seeded, diced or 1 (8-ounce)
>   can diced tomatoes
> 1 (4-ounce) can peeled, chopped, green chilies
> 2 cups (1 pound) cubed Monterey Jack cheese
> 1 (8-ounce) package cream cheese, cubed
> 1/2 pint half-and-half (1 cup)
> Salt to taste
> Hot-pepper sauce to taste
> Vegetable sticks and slices, such as bell peppers,
>   zucchini, jícama, carrots, celery, turnips and pea pods
> Corn chips

In a medium-sized heavy saucepan or deep skillet, heat butter Add onion. Sauté over low heat about 5 minutes or until soft not browned. Add tomatoes with juice and chilies. Simmer, uncovered, 15 minutes, stirring occasionally. Add Monterey Jack and cream cheese and turn heat to very lowest setting. Turn into a serving dish or pot and keep warm but do not stir. Before serving, pour in half and half and add salt and hot-pepper sauce, stirring just briefly. Offer with vegetable sticks and/or corn chips for serving. Makes about 4 cups.

Serving Suggestion: Turn dip into a heatproof pottery or glass dish and place over a candle-warmer, or into a chafing dish with a waterbath to keep dip runny during a party. Leftover dip can be kept in a covered container in the refrigerator up to 4 days, or may be frozen.

Fresh-Tomato Salsa

—•◆•—

Elena Zelayeta, the Mexican-born author, cook and teacher lived, cooked and wrote about Mexican food from her home in San Francisco. It was from her work that I first learned that Mexican food need not be blazing hot with peppers, or brick-heavy with mashed beans. This fresh-tomato sauce, an adaptation of Elena's recipe, has many uses. Serve as a dip for tortilla chips, as a topping for any Mexican-style dish, as an accompaniment to simply poached, broiled or barbecued fish or chicken, or as a side dish with roasted pork or turkey. Salsa also makes a tasty filling for an omelet.

> 3 large tomatoes, peeled, chopped (about 3 cups)
> 1/2 cup minced green onion
> 1 large green bell pepper, minced
> 1 to 3 jalapeño peppers, seeded, minced
> 1 tablespoon sugar
> 1 teaspoon salt
> 2 tablespoons minced fresh coriander or Chinese parsley
> 1/2 teaspoon dried leaf oregano
> 2 tablespoons vegetable oil
> 2 tablespoons fresh lemon or lime juice
> 1 tablespoon red-wine vinegar
> 1 (8-ounce) can tomato sauce

In a large bowl, combine all ingredients. Cover and refrigerate several hours or overnight before serving. Sauce keeps up to 5 days. Makes about 1 quart.

Guacamole

—•◆•—

An almost universal appetizer and a Mexican contribution to the flavors of the Southwest, is this avocado dip, phonetically pronounced "waca molay." It is served as a dip for crisp corn chips, but is excellent for dipping raw vegetables. Texans add Tabasco sauce and at Christmastime, scatter pomegranate seeds over the guacamole.

> 1 large ripe avocado
> 1 garlic clove, minced or pressed
> 1/4 teaspoon salt
> 1/4 teaspoon chili powder
> 2 teaspoons fresh lemon juice
> 2 teaspoons minced green onion
> 2 tablespoons diced green chilies
> 2 tablespoons sliced ripe olives
> 1 peeled seeded tomato, diced (optional)
> 3 bacon slices, cooked crisp, crumbled (optional)

Remove and discard skin and pit from avocado. In a medium-sized bowl, using a fork, mash avocado with garlic until coarse. Add salt, chili powder, lemon juice and green onion. Mix in green chilies, olives, and tomato and bacon, if desired. If made in advance, cover top of guacamole with a thin layer of mayonnaise to keep mixture from discoloring. Stir just before serving. Serve as a salad or as a dip. Makes about 2 cups.

Homemade Crackers

— ◆ —

"Crackers" are named that way because they crack. Other ethnic groups define them as a crisp, hard, thin, or flat bread. Although the name "crackers" is American, the idea is rooted in the baking tradition of every country whose people settled in the United States. And, like every food that has great acceptance, it has been produced on a commercial level to the point where the average home baker might have forgotten it is entirely possible to make crackers in her own kitchen!

> **4 cups all-purpose flour**
> **2 tablespoons sugar**
> **1 teaspoon salt**
> **1/4 cup firm butter**
> **About 1 cup milk**

Preheat oven to 425F (220C). In a large bowl, combine flour, sugar and salt. Cut in butter with a pastry blender or 2 knives until mixture resembles coarse crumbs. Stir in enough milk to make a stiff dough. On an ungreased baking sheet, roll out half of dough at a time until about 1/4 inch thick. Cut into 2-1/2-inch squares, leaving crackers in place. Prick surface with a fork and brush lightly with milk. Bake 15 to 18 minutes or until light golden in color. Makes 60 (2-1/2-inch-square) crackers.

Variations
Whole-Wheat Crackers: Substitute whole-wheat flour for all-purpose flour. Substitute dark-brown sugar for granulated sugar. Bake as above.
Sesame-Wheat Crackers: Substitute 2 cups whole-wheat flour for 2 cups all-purpose flour. Add 1/4 cup sesame seeds to mixture. Substitute honey for white sugar. Sprinkle crackers with sesame seeds after brushing with milk. Bake as above.
Caraway-Rye Crackers: Substitute 2 cups light or rye flour for 2 cups all-purpose flour. Substitute dark molasses for sugar. Add 1 teaspoon caraway seeds to mixture. Sprinkle crackers with caraway seeds after brushing with milk. Bake as above.

Old Virginia Cheddar Biscuits

— ·◆· —

For well over three centuries, Virginia has been famous for its good food and hospitality. The taverns of Williamsburg, like the taverns of London in the late 1600's played an important part in town life. Councilors and burgesses, ship captains and lawyers, merchants and planters met within tavern doors to transact business and gossip over a bottle of wine, a bowl of punch or a tankard of ale. Biscuits made rich with Cheddar cheese were offered because they were easier to make than the laborious beaten biscuits. These are, nonetheless, an excellent accompaniment to cocktails or a simple green salad. They keep well and taste best served cold.

> **1 cup all-purpose flour**
> **1/4 teaspoon salt**
> **1/3 cup (2/3 stick) firm butter**
> **1 cup (4 ounces) shredded Cheddar cheese**

Preheat oven to 350F (175C). In a medium-sized bowl, combine flour and salt. Using a pastry blender or 2 knives, cut in butter until mixture resembles coarse crumbs. Blend in cheese. Mix until dough holds together in a ball. On a lightly floured surface, roll out dough to about 1/2 inch thick. Cut with the tiniest biscuit cutter you have, even as small as 1 inch. Prick tops with a fork. Place on an ungreased baking sheet. Bake 12 to 15 minutes or until biscuits are a rich Cheddar color but not browned. Cool and store in an airtight container. Makes about 36.

Log-Cabin Cheese Straws

———————————— • ◆ • ————————————

These were offered along with a jug of wine or a tankard of beer in the Virginia taverns of old. The crisp, cheese-flavored sticks look attractive arranged piled up log-cabin-style on a platter.

    1/4 cup butter, softened
    1 cup (4 ounces) shredded sharp Cheddar Cheese
    1/4 cup milk
    1/4 teaspoon salt
    Dash of Tabasco Sauce
    1/8 teaspoon paprika
    1/8 teaspoon red (cayenne) pepper
    3/4 cup all-purpose flour
    1-1/2 cups fine soft bread crumbs
    Unbeaten egg white
    Coarse salt, grated Parmesan cheese, poppy or sesame seeds

In a large bowl, combine butter, cheese, milk, salt, Tabasco, paprika and red pepper; blend until smooth. Mix in flour and bread crumbs until blended. Refrigerate 30 minutes. Preheat oven to 350F (175C). Working with half of mixture at a time, roll out between 2 sheets of waxed paper to 1/4 inch thick. With a pastry wheel, cut into strips 5 inches long and 3/4 inch wide. Place on an ungreased baking sheet; brush with egg white, then sprinkle with salt, Parmesan cheese, poppy or sesame seeds. Bake 12 to 15 minutes or until lightly browned. Cool. Serve piled on a platter log-cabin-style. Serve as a snack with beverages or a salad. Makes about 40.

Southern Benne Biscuits

◆

African slaves who arrived in the South in the late 1600s brought benne (sesame) seeds with them. They're used in stews, cookies and pastries, and to make a crunchy benne brittle. These crackers made with benne seeds are traditionally served as a snack with a drink called *Sherry Bolo*, a mixture of sherry, lime juice and sugar.

Benne biscuits can be kept in a tightly covered jar or tin for 2 to 3 weeks. Before serving, warm and crisp for a few minutes in a low 250F (120C) oven.

> **1/2 cup benne seeds (sesame seeds)**
> **2 cups all-purpose flour**
> **1 teaspoon baking powder**
> **1/2 teaspoon salt**
> **1/2 cup butter, chilled, cut into 1/4-inch pieces**
> **1/4 cup milk**
> **Coarse kosher-style salt**

Preheat oven to 350F (175C). Spread seeds evenly on a baking sheet. Toast until golden. Remove from oven; cool. In a large bowl or in a food processor fitted with the steel blade, combine flour, baking powder and salt. Cut in butter with a pastry blender or 2 knives until mixture resembles coarse meal. Add milk. Mix until dough is smooth. If using food processor, use quick on/off pulses to cut in butter and blend in milk just until mixture is evenly moistened; don't overprocess. Mix in toasted seeds. Wrap dough. Refrigerate at least 1 hour. Cut dough in half. Shape each half into a rectangle. Place half at a time between 2 sheets of plastic wrap; roll dough paper thin. Or, roll between floured sheets of waxed paper. Gently peel off top sheet. If you have trouble, return dough to refrigerator until chilled. Cut into 1-1/2 inch rounds. Transfer to ungreased baking sheets. Reroll scraps and cut into more rounds. Bake 10 to 12 minutes or until pale golden. Sprinkle tops with coarse salt. Makes 96 (1-1/2-inch) biscuits.

Blue-Cheese Ball

◆

A blue-cheese and cream-cheese mixture shaped into a ball or roll has been a favorite appetizer spread for bread or crackers, apples and celery sticks for generations.

> **1 (8-ounce) package cream cheese, room temperature**
> **1-1/2 cups (6 ounces) crumbled blue cheese**
> **1/2 teaspoon vinegar**
> **1/2 teaspoon Dijon-style mustard**
> **Chopped peanuts**

In a food processor fitted with the steel blade or by hand, blend cream cheese, blue cheese, vinegar and mustard until smooth. Turn out onto a square of plastic wrap. Shape into a ball or a roll. Refrigerate until firm. Roll in chopped peanuts. Refrigerate until ready to serve. Makes about 1 pound.

Beer Schmierkase

—— ·◆· ——

Cheesemaking and buttermaking were part of the early colonial kitchen and went on steadily just like baking. The Shakers made a kind of cottage cheese, *schmierkase*, which they spread along with dark apple butter on slices of homemade bread.

When the process of making cheese passed onto the professionals at creameries, a wide variety developed. Today, our dairylands offer superb Cheddars, Swiss-type cheeses, soft, silky Brie, and fine blue cheeses, as well as domestic versions of Italian and French cheeses. Home cheesemaking now means "doing something" with bits and ends of cheese. This is an example of what to do with leftover cheese pieces of uneven shapes and small amounts.

2 to 3 garlic cloves, minced
1 tablespoon Worcestershire sauce
1/2 teaspoon hot-pepper sauce
1/2 teaspoon mustard powder
1/2 teaspoon salt
1 cup dark beer
4 cups (1 pound) shredded cheese, may be sharp Cheddar or a
　　combination of cheeses

In the small bowl of an electric mixer or in a food processor fitted with the steel blade, combine garlic, Worcestershire sauce, pepper sauce, mustard and salt. Slowly blend in beer, then blend in cheese, a little at a time. Beat until mixture is smooth. Pack into a 2-cup container. Cover and refrigerate overnight or longer before serving. Serve with crisp croutons or crackers, chunks of celery or wedges of crisp apple. Makes about 4 cups.

Note: Save bits and ends of cheese pieces in the freezer until you have collected enough to make this spread.

Devilled Eggs

—— ◆ ——

It was the Pennsylvania Dutch who introduced the Easter Egg and the Easter Bunny to America. At first, they tried to tell the kids that the Easter Bunny laid the eggs. They even drew pictures of rabbits laying the eggs until there was a great objection to this "stretch of the truth." But eggs continued to be the center of culinary activity during the week before Easter, Holy Week. Anybody who was raised on a farm will know that this is the time of year when the molting hens begin to lay eggs again. Households were busy dying eggs with red onion skins and other natural dyes.

At the Moravian Easter Morning church service, each worshiper received an egg marked "The Lord is Risen." A farmer, whose chicken laid an egg on Good Friday considered it a real treasure. It was to be eaten also on that day, but the shell had to be saved to drink water with on Easter Morning. Children searched for the Easter Bunny's nest where they found eggs in great quantity. There were Easter-Egg-eating contests. Eggs were made into "Easter birds" and others were stuck on an Easter-Egg tree, but most were eaten.

Here is one favorite way of preparing stuffed eggs. This might be an inspiration for anybody who has too many hard-cooked eggs on hand on Easter Sunday!

> **6 hard-cooked eggs, shelled**
> **1 teaspoon prepared mustard**
> **2 tablespoons chopped fresh parsley**
> **1 tablespoon fresh lemon juice**
> **2 tablespoons mayonnaise**
> **Salt and freshly ground black pepper to taste**
> **Paprika**

Cut eggs lengthwise into halves. Remove yolks and turn into a medium-size bowl. Mash with a fork until smooth. Blend in mustard, parsley, lemon juice, mayonnaise, salt and pepper. Spoon yolk mixture into egg whites or press through a piping bag. Sprinkle with paprika. Makes 12 servings.

Dutch Beet-Pickled Eggs

·◆·

The Pennsylvania Dutch have a great fondness for relish trays. On these attractive trays you could find cinnamon-flavored applesauce, pickled red beets, uncooked onion rings, fresh grated horseradish, chopped sweet peppers and prepared mustard. Red beet-pickled eggs capture regional relish honors. A sliced, cooked beet is used to pickle shelled, hard-cooked eggs. The red eggs appear at the table cut lengthwise into quarters, nestled in crisp celery hearts. A Dutch cook also tucks rings of them as a garnish in salads of lettuce and other greens, or inserts them in sandwiches. But, at a buffet supper, they're beautifully arranged in the best crystal bowl or platter.

2 sliced cooked beets
2 cups beet juice (from cooking beets)
2 cups red-wine vinegar
1 tablespoon mixed pickling spices
12 hard-cooked eggs, shelled

Add sliced beets to beet juice, vinegar and pickling spices in a large saucepan; heat to boiling point. Remove from heat. Add shelled hard-cooked eggs. Cool. Refrigerate 2 days or until eggs are beautifully red with a sharp zesty flavor. To serve, cut lengthwise into quarters, slices or halves. Makes 12 servings.

Peanuts Toasted in Butter

·◆·

Peanuts or "earth chocolates" were used in early Virginia as fodder for hogs, which gave the resulting meat a special flavor. Peanuts were transplanted to Africa where they were used as a cheap food on slave ships.

2 tablespoons butter
1 cup raw shelled peanuts
Salt (optional)
Red (cayenne) pepper, curry powder or seasoned salt (optional)

In a heavy skillet, heat butter over low heat. Add peanuts. Sauté 5 to 10 minutes or until toasted. Turn out onto paper towels. Sprinkle with salt and seasonings, if desired. Makes 1 cup.

Variation
Oven-Toasted Peanuts: Preheat oven to 350F (175C). Spread peanuts on a baking sheet. Bake 5 to 10 minutes or until toasted. Toss with butter in a bowl and add seasonings. Cool. Mix with an equal quantity of raisins, if desired.

Note: You can buy untoasted shelled peanuts in many groceries and in most health-food stores.

Sloppy Joes

◆

This "skilletburger" originated in the fifties, when Vitalis-slicked hair and sunglasses typified the "All-American Joe." Crumbled, cooked, ground beef served up in a hamburger bun has a tendency toward sloppiness, hence the name.

>   1 pound lean ground beef
>   1/2 cup chopped onion
>   1/2 cup chopped green bell pepper
>   1 tablespoon brown sugar
>   1 teaspoon salt
>   1/2 teaspoon paprika
>   1/4 teaspoon freshly ground black pepper
>   1 (8-ounce) can tomato sauce
>   8 to 10 hamburger buns, warmed

In a large heavy skillet over medium-high heat, cook beef with onion and green pepper, breaking up meat as it cooks. Add brown sugar, salt, paprika, black pepper and tomato sauce. Heat until bubbly. Spoon into warm hamburger buns. Fills 8 to 10 buns.

Tacos

◆

Tacos have been quickly accepted and "Americanized," probably because they offer another way of using ground beef. Originally from the Spanish-Mexican food tradition, the U-shaped crisp tortilla is filled not only with cooked ground beef but various fillings. The Mexican-Spanish meaning for the word "taco" is "wad" or "plug," which is what a snack will do to hunger pangs.

>   1 pound lean ground beef
>   1 to 3 teaspoons chili powder
>   1/2 teaspoon salt
>   1/2 teaspoon garlic salt
>   1/4 teaspoon red (cayenne) pepper
>   10 to 12 crisp taco shells
>   Cheddar cheese, shredded
>   Onion, finely chopped
>   Shredded lettuce
>   Tomatoes, finely chopped

In a large heavy skillet, crumble beef over medium heat. Add chili powder, salt, garlic salt and red pepper. Cook until meat is no longer pink. Fill each taco shell with about 2 heaping tablespoons meat filling and top with shredded cheese, onion, lettuce and tomatoes. Makes 10 to 12 tacos.

Western Sandwich

This is often called a *Denver sandwich*. It was invented by pioneers to salvage eggs that would get "high" after a long haul over hot trails. Today, we still make the sandwich, but we prefer to use fresh eggs.

1/4 pound ham or 4 bacon slices, diced
1 green bell pepper, chopped
1 medium-sized onion, chopped
4 eggs
Salt and freshly ground black pepper to taste
8 bread slices, buttered

In a large skillet, cook ham or bacon until browned. Add green pepper and onion. Cook over low heat 15 minutes or until vegetables are tender but not browned. In a medium-sized bowl, beat eggs. Add salt and pepper. Add cooked ham or bacon mixture. Spoon a quarter of egg mixture at a time into skillet to make fillings for 4 sandwiches. Cook until eggs are set and omelets are browned on both sides. Place 1 omelet between 2 slices of buttered bread. Cut into halves or quarters. Makes 4 servings.

Barbecued-Pork Sandwiches

— • ♦ • —

Barbecue is an American tradition and denotes not only the cooking of meat on an outdoor fire, but also meats that are roasted with a spicy barbecue sauce. Barbecued pork is traditional in the South and beef barbecues in the West.

Barbecue Sauce, see below
1-1/2 pounds cooked, lean, pork roast, thinly sliced
6 large hamburger buns, warmed
Dill pickles
Coleslaw with Boiled Dressing, page 120

Barbecue Sauce:
1/4 cup butter
1 cup onion, finely chopped
1 garlic clove, minced
1 cup tomato ketchup
1/2 cup dry sherry
1 tablespoon light-brown sugar
1 teaspoon mustard powder
1 tablespoon fresh lemon juice
1/2 cup white vinegar
2 teaspoons Worcestershire sauce
1/3 cup water

Preheat oven to 300F (150C). Prepare Barbecue Sauce. Combine pork and Barbecue Sauce in a 2-quart casserole, blending until slices are evenly coated. Bake, covered, 30 minutes or until pork is completely heated through. You may combine pork and sauce, cover and refrigerate until ready to heat. Add 10 to 15 minutes to heating time. Spoon heated pork and sauce onto each warm hamburger bun. Garnish with dill pickle and coleslaw, placing a heaping tablespoon of slaw on top of pork in each bun. Makes 6 servings.

To prepare Barbecue Sauce: In a medium-sized saucepan, heat butter. Add onion and garlic. Sauté over low heat 5 minutes or until onion is soft. Add remaining ingredients. Bring to a boil. Reduce heat and simmer, uncovered, 1 hour, stirring frequently to prevent scorching. Turn into a food processor fitted with the steel blade. Process until pureed. Makes 2-1/2 cups.

Barbecued Beef

—— •◆• ——

Perfect for a country lunch, this is easy to serve when you are expecting a crowd. The thin slices go into sandwich buns. The meat is even better when made ahead to be reheated before serving.

> **1/2 cup cider vinegar**
> **1 garlic clove, minced**
> **1 tablespoon vegetable oil**
> **3 tablespoons Worcestershire sauce**
> **Few drops hot-pepper sauce**
> **2 tablespoons brown sugar**
> **1 tablespoon mixed pickling spices**
> **1/2 cup tomato ketchup**
> **1 teaspoon whole-grain country-style mustard**
> **1 teaspoon salt**
> **2 to 3 pounds boneless brisket or round of beef**
> **Buttered white or rye sandwich buns**
> **Additional mustard**

In a medium-sized saucepan, combine all ingredients except meat, buns and extra mustard. Simmer, covered, 10 to 15 minutes. Preheat oven to 350F (175C). Place beef in a non-aluminum baking pan. Pour sauce over beef. Roast beef, basting with sauce frequently, about 2-1/2 hours or until meat is tender. Cool 30 minutes. Slice thinly and return to sauce. Bake 1 hour longer, turning meat in sauce frequently. Serve slices in buttered buns. Offer mustard. Makes about 6 servings per pound.

Memphis-Style Spareribs in Red Sauce

—— ·◆· ——

Memphis is famous for its barbecued spareribs. These are sometimes cooked in a charcoal smoke oven and glazed with the sauce during cooking. Roasted in the oven, the ribs also cook to tender juiciness.

4 pounds spareribs
Salt and freshly ground black pepper to taste

Red Sauce:
1 cup chopped onions
1 cup ketchup, preferably homemade
1/4 cup packed dark-brown sugar
1/4 cup cider vinegar
1/4 cup Worcestershire sauce
1 teaspoon mustard powder
1/4 teaspoon hot-pepper sauce
1/4 to 1/2 teaspoon liquid-smoke flavoring (optional)
Chopped fresh coriander or cilantro (optional)

Ask the butcher to cut the ribs crosswise. At home, with a sharp knife, cut into individual ribs. Preheat oven to 300F (150C). Sprinkle ribs with salt and pepper. Place in a baking pan in a single layer. Cover with foil. Bake 2 hours or until ribs are tender. While ribs bake, prepare Red Sauce. Drain ribs. Pour sauce over them. At this point you may put them into a deep casserole or heatproof serving dish. Cover and keep warm until ready to serve. Garnish with chopped coriander, if desired. Makes 12 to 16 appetizer servings.
To prepare Red Sauce: In a 2-quart non-aluminum saucepan, combine all ingredients except liquid-smoke flavoring, if using. Bring sauce to a boil over high heat, stirring constantly. Reduce heat to low and simmer, covered, 4 to 5 minutes or until onions are soft. Add smoke flavoring, if desired. Turn into a food processor fitted with the steel blade. Process until pureed. Makes about 3 cups.

Country Cheese Pie

◆

Cheese, which came about as a method of preserving milk, was probably one of the first manufactured foods. Reportedly it was made as early as the 15th century B.C. and is referred to in the Old Testament. There are more than 300 varieties of cheese being made in the United States today. Although the original cheesemaking in America was developed from English traditions, many varieties indigenous to us reflect tastes from many countries in the world. Colby, for instance, is a cheese first made by the Steinwand family in Colby, Wisconsin at the end of the 19th century. Monterey Jack cheese originated in Monterey, California, and was developed by David Jacks after the Gold Rush years. It resembled cheese made by early Spanish friars and today is essential in Mexican-American cookery. Fresh cheeses, such as cottage cheese, farmer's cheese or pot cheeses were made by just about every dairy farmer. The Pennsylvania Dutch loved cheese but rarely used it in cooking except for cheese cake and cheese pie, which are basically the same.

Crust:
1 cup all-purpose flour
1/2 cup butter
2 tablespoons milk
Pinch *each* of salt and sugar
1 tablespoon Dijon-style mustard

Filling:
3 tablespoons butter
1 cup thinly sliced green onions, including tops
4 eggs, slightly beaten
1-1/3 cups half and half
1 cup diced mild, medium or sharp Cheddar cheese, cut into
    1/2-inch dice
1 cup (4 ounces) shredded white cheese such as Swiss, Jack,
    Brick or white Cheddar

Measure flour into a medium-sized bowl. Using a pastry blender or 2 knives, cut in butter until mixture resembles coarse crumbs. Add milk, salt and sugar, tossing with a fork until dough holds together in a ball. Wrap and refrigerate 30 minutes before rolling out. Preheat oven to 400F (205C). On a lightly floured board, roll out dough to fit a 9" x 1" quiche or tart pan generously. Carefully fit into pan. Trim dough edge 1 inch larger than pan. Fold 3/4 inch under and press firmly against sides of pan. Line dough with foil or waxed paper; fill with uncooked beans, rice or pie weights. Bake 12 to 15 minutes or until edge of crust is slightly golden. Lift out foil or paper with weights. Cool. Brush bottom of pastry with mustard.
To prepare Filling: In a small skillet, heat butter. Add green onions. Sauté 5 minutes over medium heat, stirring constantly. Remove from heat and sprinkle into bottom of crust. In a medium-sized bowl, combine eggs and half and half. Sprinkle Cheddar-cheese cubes in crust over green onions. Top with shredded cheese. Pour egg mixture over. Bake 30 to 40 minutes or until pie is set. Makes 8 to 10 appetizer servings.

–VEGETABLES & SIDE DISHES–

Vegetables have been historically short-changed and if they have been served, it has usually been in an overcooked state, hardly dressed but with salt and pepper and perhaps butter. We do have a few classics such as Harvard Beets which became popular mostly because beets grow well in gardens. Country cooks will can beets into beet pickles and reserve a few without the brine to heat and season later. The other classic American vegetables are corn, beans, potatoes and squash.

The potato, a native of the highlands of Ecuador and Peru, still grows wild today. The Spaniards brought the potato to North America, but it was also brought to New Hampshire from Ireland in 1719.

The lowly potato is probably the most universally accepted vegetable today. Originally there was just one variety but today through careful breeding and cultivation we have many varieties of boiling and baking potatoes.

One evening in 1853, George Crum, chef at a Saratoga Springs, New York, resort received a complaint that his French fries were too thick. Amused, he shaved some paper-thin slices of potato, fried them and sent them out to the dining room. To his amazement, customers were delighted with this new snack. "Saratoga Chips" became known in the region.

It took another half century for the chips to develop national popularity. In 1918, Marcus Nalley, a chef in an Idaho resort began packaging and delivering "Nalley's Saratoga chips" in the Northwest. Three years later, Earl Wise, a small town Pennsylvania grocer, overstocked with potatoes, began making and marketing "Wise Potato Chips."

In the early years of the Great Depression, Herman W. Lay began selling potato chips in the hills of Tennessee for his financially troubled snack-food firm. A few years later he bought an Atlanta-based company. In 1939, H. W. Lay & Company was founded, and "Lay's Potato Chips" were born.

Potatoes au Gratin

— ◆ —

"Au gratin" denotes a topping of buttered crumbs or cheese or both. Although this sounds French, it is all-American!

> 1/2 cup butter
> 1/4 cup sliced green onions
> 1/2 cup chopped green bell pepper
> 1 (2-ounce) jar chopped pimiento, undrained
> 1 teaspoon salt
> 1/4 teaspoon freshly ground black pepper
> 1 tablespoon chopped fresh parsley
> 1 teaspoon paprika
> 6 tablespoons all-purpose flour
> 1 quart milk (4 cups)
> 6 cups cubed cooked potatoes
> 2 cups (8 ounces) shredded sharp Cheddar cheese

Preheat oven to 350F (175C). Grease a shallow 3-quart baking dish. In a large heavy skillet, heat butter. Add green onions, green pepper and pimiento. Sauté 1 minute. Add salt, black pepper, parsley, paprika and flour; stir until blended. Stir in milk and cook, stirring, until thickened. Add cooked potatoes and 1 cup cheese. Stir until cheese is melted. Pour mixture into greased dish. Sprinkle with remaining cheese. Bake 30 to 45 minutes or until bubbly. Makes 10 to 12 servings.

Hash-Browned Potatoes

— ◆ —

The white potato is native to South America and was cultivated thousands of years ago in Peru. The Spanish explorers found the Incas cultivating this tuber and called it *patata*. The Incan name was "papa." The potato arrived in North America via Europe and was one of the earliest of the cultivated crops of the new settlers in New England. This is a "hash-house favorite."

> **3 cups diced cooked or raw potatoes**
> **Salt and freshly ground black pepper to taste**
> **1/4 cup minced onion (optional)**
> **1/4 cup minced fresh parsley or fresh spinach (optional)**
> **1/4 cup half and half (optional)**
> **2 to 4 tablespoons butter or bacon drippings**

In a large bowl, combine potatoes, salt and pepper, onion and parsley or spinach, if used. Stir in half and half, if used. In a slope-sided, preferably nonstick skillet, heat 2 tablespoons butter or drippings. Add potatoes. Cook over medium heat until potatoes are browned and bottom is crusty, lifting potatoes at first until they are well-coated with fat. Reduce heat and cook until potatoes are tender, if using raw potatoes. Add more fat, if necessary, to keep potatoes from sticking. Slide potatoes out onto a plate, then invert and slide from plate back into skillet, browned-side up. Brown 5 to 10 minutes, shaking skillet constantly. Slide out onto a warm platter. Cut into wedges to serve. Makes 6 servings.

Old-Fashioned Scalloped Potatoes

— ◆ —

Many a farm girl learned to prepare scalloped potatoes without a recipe. She was told to plan on one potato per person and to vary the number of servings by the size of the baking dish. She would plan on four large potatoes per quart size of the baking dish. Here is the country-style recipe.

Preheat oven to 325F (165C). Grease a baking dish of the appropriate size. Pare potatoes, using 1 per person and 1 extra. Place a layer of potatoes in greased baking dish; sprinkle with a little flour. Sprinkle with salt, pepper and some chopped onion. Dot with butter. Layer potatoes and seasonings until dish is full or within a half inch of the top. Pour in enough milk to reach top layer. New potatoes tend to be more acidic causing milk to curdle, so if using them, substitute cream or undiluted evaporated milk. Bake 1-1/2 hours or until tender. A 1-quart baking dish yields 4 servings.

Twice-Baked Potatoes

—— • ◆ • ——

Not just a side dish anymore, these potatoes are stuffed with enough to make them a main dish for a light supper or lunch! Of course, if you wish to serve them with an old-fashioned roast-beef dinner, you can. But plan on hearty eaters! You'll love the convenience of being able to make these potatoes ahead, refrigerate or freeze, and bake them just before serving.

> **4 large white Idaho Russet potatoes**
> **3/4 cup whipping cream or half-and-half**
> **1/4 cup butter**
> **1/2 cup chopped onion**
> **Salt and freshly ground black pepper to taste**
> **1 cup (4 ounces) shredded sharp Cheddar cheese**

Preheat oven to 450F (230C). Scrub potatoes; pierce each with a fork. Bake 1 hour or until potatoes test done. Scald cream or half and half by heating almost to boiling point. Meanwhile, heat butter in a skillet. Add onion. Sauté over low to medium heat 5 minutes or until onion is translucent. Remove potatoes from oven. Cool until you can touch them. Cut potatoes lengthwise in halves and scoop out pulp into the large bowl of an electric mixer. Mash potatoes. Add onion, hot cream or half and half, salt and pepper. Beat until smooth and fluffy. Pile whipped potato mixture back into potato shells. Top with shredded cheese. You may at this point refrigerate or freeze the potatoes until ready to serve. To serve, preheat oven to 350F (175C). Bake 15 to 20 minutes or until heated through and cheese is melted. If frozen, thaw before heating. Makes 8 servings.

Oven Fries

—— • ◆ • ——

Try these with the Oven-Fried Chicken, page 40

> **6 medium-sized potatoes, not pared**
> **Melted butter or vegetable oil**
> **Salt and freshly ground black pepper to taste**

Preheat oven to 375F (190C). Scrub potatoes. Dry and cut into quarters lengthwise. Brush with melted butter or oil. Sprinkle with salt and pepper. Line a baking sheet with foil. Place potatoes on baking sheet. If desired, bake along with Oven-Fried Chicken 50 minutes or until potatoes are tender. Makes 6 servings.

Sweet-Potato Bake

Wild roots were an important source of food for the early settlers. Not the least of these sources was the sweet potato, commonly called a *yam* although it isn't one. This golden tuber belongs to the morning-glory family and grow wild in the South. Yams are the starchy, tuberous, root of any number of climbing vines. Although both are available, they can be used interchangeably in various recipes calling for sweet potatoes or yams. A food first discovered and eaten by the Indians, sweet potatoes or yams were part of the original Thanksgiving menu and have remained a standard menu item ever since.

3 to 4 sweet potatoes or yams (about 3 pounds)
1/4 cup packed brown sugar
1/2 cup butter
1/2 cup bourbon, sherry or orange juice

Preheat oven to 350F (175C). Grease a baking dish. Boil sweet potatoes or yams in their jackets until a wooden pick can be inserted into vegetables with a little resistance, but not until mushy. Peel and cut into large chunks. Place in greased baking dish. Sprinkle with sugar; dot with butter. Pour bourbon, sherry or orange juice over. Bake, uncovered, 30 to 40 minutes or until browned and bubbly. Makes 6 servings.

Variations
Pecan-Sweet-Potato Bake: Top Sweet-Potato Bake, above, with 1 cup pecan halves before baking.
Ambrosia Sweet-Potato Bake: Slice cooked sweet potatoes or yams. Alternate layers of sliced potatoes with a half each of a peeled sliced lemon and orange, and 1 (8-ounce) can crushed pineapple in unsweetened pineapple juice, undrained. Add brown sugar and butter as directed above but omit bourbon, sherry or orange juice. Top with 1/2 cup shredded or flaked coconut. Bake as above.
Sweet Potatoes Supreme: Whip cooked potatoes and whip in brown sugar and softened butter, along with 2 eggs, 3 tablespoons all-purpose flour, 1/2 cup whipping cream, 1 teaspoon lemon extract and 1 teaspoon vanilla extract. Turn into a greased 1-1/2-quart shallow baking dish. Top with about 1/2 cup pecan halves. Bake at 325F (165C) 1 hour.

Squash with Maple Syrup

—•◆•—

Butternut and blue hubbard squashes when baked, mashed and topped with a bit of "spring magic"—maple syrup, make an irresistible dish. September, October, November and December are the months for butternut squash, though early in November it reaches its peak. After Thanksgiving Day the squash rapidly loses quality and that's when New England cooks freeze a supply of it cooked and mashed.

2 pounds hubbard squash or any yellow winter squash
Butter
Salt and freshly ground black pepper to taste
Maple syrup

Preheat oven to 300F (150C). Cut squash into 4 equal pieces, removing seeds and stringy parts. Place in a casserole with a cover. Bake, covered, 2 hours or until soft. Remove squash flesh from shell. Mash and season to taste with butter, salt, pepper and maple syrup. Makes 4 servings.

Cream-Fried Tomatoes

———————————————————— • ◆ • ————————————————————

This dish may be made with green tomatoes when they are available, otherwise use firm red tomatoes.

4 large firm tomatoes
1 teaspoon salt
Freshly ground black pepper to taste
1/2 cup all-purpose flour
6 tablespoons butter
2 tablespoons brown sugar
1/2 pint whipping cream (1 cup)
1 tablespoon finely chopped fresh parsley

Slice tomatoes 1/2 inch thick, discarding bottom and top ends. Sprinkle slices with salt and pepper. Dip in flour, coating each side thoroughly and gently shaking off any excess. In a large, heavy, preferably nonstick skillet, heat butter. Add tomato slices. Cook about 5 minutes or until browned. Sprinkle with half of brown sugar. Carefully turn tomatoes over and sprinkle with remaining brown sugar. Cook 3 to 4 minutes, then transfer slices to a warm serving platter. Pour cream into skillet. Increase heat to high and bring cream to a boil, stirring constantly. Boil rapidly 2 to 3 minutes or until cream thickens. Taste and adjust for seasoning, then pour sauce over tomatoes. Sprinkle with parsley. Makes 4 to 6 servings.

Harvard Beets

———————————————————— • ◆ • ————————————————————

This "educated" beet preparation is a favorite, and presumably was first prepared in the kitchens of Harvard University.

1 pound fresh uncooked beets or 1 (16-ounce) can sliced beets
2 tablespoons cider vinegar
1 tablespoon cornstarch
2 tablespoons sugar
Dash of salt
1 tablespoon chopped crystallized ginger
2 tablespoons butter

Cook fresh beets in water to cover until they "give" with pressure. Cool; slip off skins. Slice. Measure 3/4 cup beet cooking broth, or reserve 3/4 cup from canned beets. In a medium-sized heavy saucepan, combine beet broth with vinegar, cornstarch, sugar, salt and ginger. Cook, stirring, over low heat until thickened. Add beets and heat through. Stir in butter before serving. Makes 4 servings.

Fried Green Tomatoes

— ◆ • —

The lowly tomato has unworthily endured a bad reputation over the span of history. Native to South America, it was brought back to Europe by Spanish explorers early in the 16th century. Having been described as everything from unhealthy to poisonous, the "love apple" became known as an exotic vegetable. Later it was botanically classified as a fruit.

Thomas Jefferson, the "gourmet president," grew tomatoes in his garden in 1782. In the early 1800s there was only one variety of tomato seed available. They have since been bred for all purposes and there are hundreds of varieties being grown today. Anybody who has a garden with tomatoes does, however, at the close of the season end up with unripened green tomatoes. They can be made into pickles, relishes and preserves as the Pennsylvania Dutch and Shakers do, or they can be sliced and fried.

6 large green tomatoes
1/2 cup fine dry bread crumbs
1 tablespoon sugar
1/2 teaspoon freshly ground black pepper
1/2 cup all-purpose flour
1 egg, beaten
Butter

Slice tomatoes 1/2 inch thick. Place in a medium-sized bowl. Add cold salted water to cover. Soak 1 hour; drain. Combine bread crumbs, sugar and pepper on a plate. Coat drained tomato slices first with flour, then dip in egg and then in bread-crumb mixture. In a large heavy skillet, heat butter. Add tomato slices. Cook 4 to 5 minutes or until golden on both sides. Makes 6 servings.

Finnish Rutabaga Casserole

— ◆ • —

Finns always serve this rutabaga casserole with holiday meals. Rutabagas are deep-yellow root vegetables that grow well in northern climates. They are similar, but stronger in taste than a turnip.

6 cups diced peeled rutabagas (about 2 medium-sized)
1/2 cup whipping cream
1 teaspoon salt
1/2 teaspoon freshly grated nutmeg
2 eggs, beaten
3 tablespoons butter

Grease a 2-1/2- to 3-quart baking dish. Put rutabagas in a 3-quart pot and add water to cover. Bring to a boil. Reduce heat and simmer about 20 minutes or until tender. Drain and mash. Stir in cream, salt, nutmeg and eggs. Preheat oven to 350F (175C). Turn rutabaga mixture into greased dish. Dot top with butter. Bake 1 hour or until lightly browned. Makes 6 to 8 servings.

Virginia Fresh-Corn Pudding

— ◆ —

This is more of a soufflé than a pudding and it makes an excellent main dish for Sunday brunch, served with a fresh-from-the-garden green salad. You can make this with frozen or canned corn but do try the taste of fresh corn in this pudding!

3 large ears fresh corn, husked, or 1-1/4 cups whole-kernel
    corn, frozen or canned, drained
3 eggs, separated
2 tablespoons butter
2 tablespoons cornstarch
1 cup milk
2 teaspoons sugar
1/2 teaspoon salt

Preheat oven to 400F (205C). Grease a 1-quart soufflé dish. With a sharp knife, slit each row of corn lengthwise through the center. Slice corn off cob in thin slices. In a large bowl, stir egg yolks and add corn; blend well. In a small saucepan, heat butter. Add cornstarch. Whisk in milk. Bring to a boil. Cook, stirring, until sauce is smooth and thickened. Stir in sugar and salt. Gradually stir hot sauce into corn mixture. In a large bowl, whip egg whites until stiff. Fold into corn mixture. Turn mixture into greased dish. Bake 25 to 30 minutes or until pudding is browned on top but still jiggles a little when tapped on the side. Serve immediately. Makes 4 servings.

Succotash

— ◆ —

The Indians planted beans on the same hill with corn so the vines of one might run up the stalks of the other. After the harvest, they boiled the two vegetables together to blend the juices. They called the dish *succotash*. "Succotash" is a shortening of the Narragansett Indian name "M'Sickquatash" which is corn boiled whole without crushing or grinding.

2 tablespoons butter
2 cups cooked lima or kidney beans
2 cups corn, scraped fresh from the cob, or frozen whole-kernel
    corn, or drained, canned, whole-kernel corn
1/2 cup water
1/2 teaspoon salt
1/8 teaspoon freshly ground black pepper
1 teaspoon sugar
1/4 cup whipping cream

In a large saucepan, heat butter. Add beans, corn, water, salt, pepper and sugar. Cook, covered, over low heat about 15 minutes or until water is absorbed. Stir in cream. Reheat and serve hot. Makes 6 servings.

Fresh-Corn Fritters

◆ • ◆

Old-fashioned corn fritters are made with just the simplest of ingredients, fresh corn, flour and beaten eggs. A dash of salt brings out the flavor but is not necessary. These are great made in tiny puffs and served hot from the fryer. Although the fritters can be made with frozen or canned corn, there is nothing quite like the fresh flavor of corn straight from the field!

> **6 ears fresh corn, husked, or 2-1/2 cups whole-kernel corn,**
>   **frozen or canned, drained**
> **3 eggs, well-beaten**
> **About 1/2 cup all-purpose flour**
> **Dash of salt (optional)**
> **Hot fat, preferably half oil, half butter**

With a sharp knife, slit each row of corn lengthwise through the center. Slice corn off cob in thin slices into a medium-sized bowl. Blend well-beaten eggs with corn. Fold in enough flour to make a batter that is still fluffy but with a consistency that will hold together when dropped into hot fat. Add salt, if desired. In a large heavy skillet or deep-fat fryer, heat fat to about 375F (190C) or until a 1-inch cube of bread turns golden brown in 50 seconds. Drop batter by spoonfuls into fat and fry until golden on both sides, about 1-1/2 minutes in all. Remove and drain. Serve hot. To keep hot and crispy, place fritters on a baking sheet and hold in a warm (300F, 150C) oven until ready to serve, no more than 30 minutes. Makes about 30 fritters.

Buttermilk-Fried Onions

— • ◆ • —

Large, crispy, deep-fried onion rings are an American classic, especially in small diners and hamburger joints. They probably originated in the South. Unfortunately, these mouth-watering morsels are not a low-calorie snack!

Hot fat
2 egg yolks
3/4 cup all-purpose flour
1/4 teaspoon baking soda
3/4 teaspoon salt
1/2 pint buttermilk (1 cup)
4 large yellow onions, cut into 1/4-inch crosswise rings

In a large heavy skillet or deep-fat fryer, heat fat to 375F (190C) or until a 1-inch cube of bread turns golden brown in 50 seconds. In a medium-sized bowl, whisk together egg yolks, flour, baking powder, salt and buttermilk. Dip onion rings into batter. Drop into hot fat and fry 4 to 5 minutes or until crisp on both sides. Drain and serve immediately. Makes about 8 servings.

Other Classic American Onion Dishes:
Grilled Onions: Slice onions thinly and sauté on a grill or in a heavy skillet along with hamburgers, steaks, chops or chicken. Serve them on top of the meat.
Connecticut Onions: Peel onions and boil whole in water to cover until tender. Drain and season with salt and pepper. Pour over enough whipping cream just to moisten outside of onions. Serve immediately.
Milton Onions: Prepare as for Connecticut Onions, above, but top with shredded Cheddar or Jack cheese. Broil until cheese is melted.

Note: Cowboys used to call onions "skunk eggs."

Red Cabbage & Apples

· ◆ ·

Red cabbage is classic to many nationalities. It is often part of the holiday menu and is served with baked ham, roast pork, goose or meatballs.

   1 (2- to 3-pound) head red cabbage
   1/4 cup butter
   2 medium-sized onions, chopped
   4 medium-sized tart apples, sliced
   1 teaspoon salt
   1/2 teaspoon freshly ground black pepper
   1/4 teaspoon ground allspice
   2 tablespoons red-wine vinegar
   1/4 cup water
   3 tablespoons sugar
   1-1/2 cups red wine or apple juice

Preheat oven to 375F (190C). Shred cabbage. In a Dutch oven or ovenproof skillet, heat butter. Add cabbage. Sauté 5 minutes over medium heat, turning cabbage over constantly. Add onions, apples, salt, pepper and allspice. Cook 3 minutes over medium heat. Add vinegar, water, sugar and wine or apple juice. Bake, covered, 1 hour. Makes 6 to 8 servings.

Fancy Mushroom Scallop

The fear of mushroom poisoning has inhibited us from developing an interest in wild mushrooms, though we have many delicious edible varieties. Consequently, cultivated mushrooms are the most common. This is a simple and favorite way to serve cultivated or wild mushrooms as a vegetable.

2 tablespoons butter
1-1/2 pounds fresh mushrooms, sliced
3 tablespoons all-purpose flour
1/4 cup chopped fresh parsley
1-1/4 cups whipping cream
1 tablespoon fresh lemon juice
Dash of paprika
1/2 teaspoon salt
1 egg yolk
1 cup cracker crumbs

Preheat oven to 350F (175C). In a large heavy skillet, heat butter. Add mushrooms. Sauté 2 minutes or until heated through. Sprinkle with flour; add parsley. Cook, stirring, until flour is absorbed. Add 1 cup cream. Simmer 10 minutes. Stir in lemon juice, paprika and salt. Remove from heat. In a small bowl, beat egg yolk with remaining cream. Stir into mushroom mixture. Pour into a shallow 1-quart baking dish. Sprinkle with cracker crumbs. Bake 45 to 55 minutes or until golden. Makes 6 servings.

Peas & Steamed Dumplings

On the Northeastern dinner table, peas retain their position of honor in the Fourth of July dinner, along with boiled salmon. Most cooks keep two groups of recipes, one for the tender young seeds in green pods and the other for the end-of-the season peas. The more mature peas go into soup and this delicious entree. Dumplings are steamed on top of the cooked peas. The dish signifies "the last of the pea season."

1 cup all-purpose flour
1-1/2 teaspoons baking powder
1/2 teaspoon salt
1 egg, slightly beaten
1/3 cup milk
1/4 cup chopped fresh parsley
1 pound shelled peas, fresh or frozen
1 cup chicken broth or water

In a medium-sized bowl, combine flour, baking powder and salt. Add egg, milk and parsley; stir to blend well. Place peas and broth or water in a Dutch oven. Bring to a boil over high heat. Drop batter by rounded teaspoons onto peas and broth. Simmer, covered, over low heat 15 minutes. Serve dumplings alongside peas. Makes 4 servings.

Boovashenkel

◆

This potato dumpling is an old Pennsylvania Dutch specialty. It makes a perfect side dish with ham. Accompany with a dandelion salad to be authentic!

> **2 eggs**
> **About 1 cup all-purpose flour**
> **1/2 teaspoon salt**
> **1-1/2 cups mashed potatoes**
> **1 egg, beaten**
> **2 onions, chopped**
> **1 tablespoon minced fresh parsley**
> **Salt and pepper to taste**
> **2 slices ham (about 1-1/2 pounds)**
> **Additional chopped fresh parsley**

In a large bowl, or in a food processor fitted with the steel blade, beat 2 eggs. Blend in as much flour as eggs will moisten. Add 1/2 teaspoon salt. On a floured surface, roll out dough until very thin. Cut into 6-inch circles. In a large bowl, combine mashed potatoes, egg, onions and parsley. Add salt and pepper. Place a heaping tablespoonful of potato mixture onto each dough round. Fold over and moisten edges; pinch to seal. Heat about 2 quarts water to boiling in a large kettle; add 2 tablespoons salt. Drop stuffed dumplings into boiling water. Simmer gently, uncovered, 12 minutes. In a large heavy skillet, fry ham until heated through. Place on a warm platter. Surround ham with dumplings. Sprinkle with chopped parsley. Makes 6 servings.

◆ SALADS & RELISHES ◆

A "salad" to an American brings to mind a bowl of ruffled lettuces and other crisp, bright-colored vegetable ingredients. To make a salad, according to one old cookbook, you don't need a recipe. You just go to the garden and gather lettuce, radishes, onions, spinach, baby carrots and other handy vegetables and toss them in a bowl. Then you drench it with oil and vinegar and sprinkle it with salt and pepper. That's probably what Thomas Jefferson did, who loved salads and grew 19 or more varieties of greens in his Monticello gardens. Such latitude proves the statement that "there can always be a salad."

Indeed, each ethnic group had its basic "no-recipe" salad that was concocted by "taste and touch." With the Pennsylvania Dutch it was a cabbage "slaw" made with either a boiled dressing or using bacon fat in place of oil. The Shakers made fruit salads, the Germans potato salad, Italians made antipasto, and others made salads including starches like pasta.

When flavored gelatin hit the market in 1902, a whole era of shimmering "salads" became popular. Once when I was touring the Kraft company in Chicago, a salesman, spotting my identity from "northern Minnesota," asked me, "What do you do in your part of the country to use all those marshmallows? We sell more marshmallows in northern Minnesota than anywhere else in the country!" This being the late fifties, and having spent several afternoons at 4-H picnics, I answered, "They put them into lime gelatin for a salad."

Country-style relishes and pickles have a similarity to salads in that the ingredients are much the same, except they have been pickled and preserved. Grandma called it "putting summer into a jar." Any vegetable that comes up excess at the end of the summer's garden is likely to have its relish recipe. Corn relish, zucchini, canned tomatoes, tomato ketchups and cucumber pickles keep the gardener-cook busy late into the fall. The heritage of relishes seems to stem back to the Pennsylvania Dutch. They kept busy packing away garden produce to augment winter meals with their classic "seven sweets and seven sours" which were required for holiday and Sunday gatherings.

Coleslaw with Boiled Dressing

—— •◆• ——

"Slau" is Dutch for salad. "Kholslau" became "coldslaw" which became "coleslaw," and was the favorite Dutch way to prepare fresh cabbage. Original "slau" had only cabbage in it but as the recipe has evolved, innumerable variations using everything from other vegetables to fruits and nuts are now common as part of the mixture. This old-fashioned dressing was popular before the mayonnaise we use today.

Boiled Dressing, see below
1 pound firm white cabbage
2 large carrots, shredded

Boiled Dressing:
1/4 cup cider vinegar
1/4 cup water
1 tablespoon sugar
1 tablespoon all-purpose flour
1 teaspoon mustard powder
1 teaspoon salt
1/4 cup whipping cream
1 tablespoon butter
2 eggs

Prepare Boiled Dressing; cover and cool. Trim core and outer leaves from cabbage. Shred remaining cabbage finely. Toss with carrots in bowl with dressing. Cover and refrigerate 2 to 3 hours before serving. Makes 6 servings.

To prepare Boiled Dressing: In a 2-quart saucepan, combine vinegar, water, sugar, flour, mustard and salt. Stir with a wire whisk until mixture is smooth. Place over medium heat. Add cream and butter, stirring constantly with a whisk. Cook, stirring, until butter melts and sauce begins to simmer. In a small bowl, whisk eggs. Stir a small amount of hot sauce into eggs. Return entire mixture to saucepan. Reduce heat to low and cook until dressing thickens. Turn into a serving bowl. Makes about 1 cup.

Napa-Cabbage Salad

·◆·

Another good dish to accompany Oven-Fried Chicken, page 40.

4 cups shredded Napa cabbage
1 green bell pepper, sliced
1/2 cup shredded carrots

Dressing:
1/2 cup sugar
1/2 cup cider vinegar
1/4 cup vegetable oil
1 teaspoon salt

In a large salad bowl, toss vegetables together. Prepare Dressing. Pour over vegetables; toss until coated. Makes 6 servings.
To prepare Dressing: In a small bowl, combine all ingredients. Makes 3/4 cup.

Cauliflower Slaw

·◆·

Cauliflower, another member of the cabbage family, makes an excellent slaw. Broccoli and shredded Brussels sprouts may also be used in place of part of the cauliflower.

3 cups thinly sliced cauliflower
1 green bell pepper, sliced
1 red bell pepper, sliced
1 medium-sized sweet onion, sliced into rings

Dressing:
1/2 cup sugar
1/2 cup cider vinegar
1/4 cup vegetable oil
1 teaspoon salt

In a large salad bowl, toss vegetables together. Prepare Dressing. Pour over vegetables; toss until coated. Marinate at least 1 hour before serving; refrigerate if marinating more than 1 hour. Makes 6 to 8 servings.
To prepare Dressing: In a small bowl, combine all ingredients. Makes about 3/4 cup.

Harriet's German Potato Salad

This is a wonderful potato salad with an unusual marinade which can be used again on another salad. Team it with bratwurst and rye buns for a terrific picnic meal.

6 medium-sized potatoes, pared, sliced

Marinade:
2 green onions, chopped
1 bunch parsley, minced
1 (10-3/4-ounce) can concentrated chicken broth, undiluted
1 tablespoon whole-grain German-style mustard
1/4 cup cider vinegar
1/2 cup olive oil
1 teaspoon salt
Freshly ground black pepper to taste

Put sliced potatoes into a medium-sized saucepan. Add water to cover. Bring to a boil. Reduce heat and simmer 20 minutes or until potatoes are just tender; drain and place in a serving bowl. Prepare Marinade. Pour over hot drained potatoes. Carefully mix so potatoes do not break up. Cover and refrigerate overnight. Drain marinade before serving. Makes 6 servings.

To prepare Marinade: In a small bowl, combine marinade ingredients until blended.

Marinated Garbanzo Beans

Add this great salad to a barbecue menu. Garbanzo beans or chick peas are a contribution of the Italian, Greek, Spanish and Basque cultures to American cuisine.

    2 (16-ounce) cans garbanzo beans or chick peas
    1 cup diced celery
    1 green bell pepper, cut into 1/2-inch dice
    Marinade, see below
    Crisp salad greens
    Radishes
    Tomatoes

    Marinade:
    1/2 cup olive oil
    1/2 cup red-wine vinegar
    1/4 cup chopped fresh parsley
    1/4 cup chopped green onions
    1 small garlic clove, minced or pressed
    1 tablespoon capers
    1 teaspoon *each* dried leaf basil, dried leaf tarragon, chili
      powder and sugar
    Dash of hot-pepper sauce
    1/2 teaspoon salt

Drain garbanzo beans. In a medium-sized bowl, combine garbanzo beans, celery and green pepper. Prepare Marinade. Pour over bean mixture. Mix until blended. Place crisp greens in a serving bowl. Arrange bean mixture over greens. Garnish as desired with radishes and tomatoes. Makes 8 servings.

To prepare Marinade: In a small bowl, combine marinade ingredients until blended.

Shaker Green-Bean Salad

♦

The Shakers advocated the use of herbs in cookery because "they stimulate appetite and give character to food." In the summer when the green beans and fresh herbs are in the garden and the flower beds have spicy nasturtiums in bloom, it is the perfect time to make this beautiful salad.

> 1 teaspoon sugar
> 1/2 pound green beans, cut into 1-1/2-inch lengths
> Dressing, see below
> 2 quarts fresh garden lettuce, cut into 1-inch pieces
> 12 nasturtium blossoms (optional)
> 2 tablespoons chopped green onion
>
> *Dressing:*
> 3 tablespoons tarragon-flavored vinegar
> 1 tablespoon chopped green onion
> 1/2 teaspoon *each* dried leaf thyme, dried leaf summer savory
>   and salt
> 2 teaspoons whole-grain country-style mustard
> Freshly ground black pepper to taste
> 1/2 cup olive, walnut, or vegetable oil

Fill a medium-sized saucepan half-full with water. Bring to a boil; add sugar. Drop green beans into boiling water. Boil 3 to 4 minutes or just until beans are bright green. Drain and chill immediately in cold water; drain. Prepare Dressing. Add drained beans; let stand 30 minutes. Immediately before serving, arrange lettuce in a serving bowl. Top with beans, including dressing. Garnish with nasturtium blossoms, if desired. Sprinkle with 2 tablespoons green onion. Makes 4 to 6 servings.

To prepare Dressing: In a medium-sized bowl, combine vinegar, 1 tablespoon green onion, thyme, summer savory, salt, mustard and pepper. Whisk in oil until blended. Makes 2/3 cup.

Pennsylvania Dutch Dandelion Salad

If you are in southeastern Pennsylvania early in the spring or late in the winter, you might still see men, women and children carrying baskets and stooping over as if looking for something. They are in search of tender, young, dandelion greens before the plants bloom. On Maundy Thursday before Easter, the Pennsylvania Dutch always have something green on the table to ensure good health for the remainder of the year. Dandelion salad fills this need. They insist the best hot dressing for dandelion greens contains cream or rich milk.

> 2 quarts young dandelion greens or fresh young spinach,
>   washed, dried
> 4 bacon slices
> Dressing, see below
> Chopped hard-cooked eggs
>
> *Dressing:*
> 1/2 cup whipping cream
> 1/4 cup cider vinegar
> 1/4 cup sugar
> 1 tablespoon all-purpose flour
> Dash of salt

Put dandelion greens in a serving bowl. In a heavy skillet, slowly cook bacon until crisp. Remove to a hot plate and crumble; set aside. Prepare Dressing. Pour over greens. Garnish with bacon and chopped hard-cooked egg. Makes 4 to 6 servings.

To prepare Dressing: Add cream, vinegar, sugar, flour and salt to bacon drippings in skillet. Bring dressing to a boil, stirring constantly. Makes about 3/4 cup.

President Jefferson Salad

From all reports, President Jefferson knew good food. He loved salads of "mixed garden stuff." In his garden at Monticello he grew 19 varieties of lettuce alone!

Jefferson took a great interest in sesame oil as a substitute for salad oil. On January 6, 1808, he wrote from Monticello to John Taylor of South Carolina: "The Africans brought over to Georgia a seed they called Beni, and the botanists Sesamum. I lately received a bottle of the oil, which was eaten with salad by various companies. All agree it is equal to the olive oil, a bushel of seed yields 3 gallons of oil. I propose to cultivate it for my own use at least." *(American Heritage Cookbook).*

1 head Bibb lettuce
1 bunch watercress
1 small head curly endive
1 small head iceberg lettuce
1 small head chicory
1 cup fresh spinach leaves
1 tablespoon chopped chives

Monticello Dressing:
1 small garlic clove, minced or pressed
1 teaspoon salt
1/2 teaspoon white pepper
1/3 cup olive oil
1/3 cup sesame oil
1/3 cup tarragon-flavored or wine vinegar

Wash all greens in cold water; drain and dry. Tear, don't cut, into bite-sized pieces. Combine in a serving bowl. Refrigerate to crisp. Prepare Monticello Dressing. Immediately before serving, toss salad with shaken dressing. Makes 6 to 8 servings
To prepare Monticello Dressing: Combine all ingredients in a jar with a lid. Shake well before pouring over salad greens. Makes 1 cup.

Waldorf Salad

— ◆ —

When this salad was created, it was made only with apples, celery and mayonnaise. Walnuts were added to the recipe later. Reportedly, this salad was first served by and named after an old New York landmark, the ritzy Waldorf Astoria Hotel and became a standard item on restaurant menus. Waldorf salad also showed up at country picnics and is a standard at apple festivals today.

> **3 large firm apples, cored, diced**
> **2 tablespoons fresh lemon juice**
> **3 celery stalks, diced**
> **1 cup coarsely chopped walnuts**
> **1 cup mayonnaise**
> **1/2 cup dairy sour cream**
> **Fresh lettuce leaves**
> **Fresh watercress or parsley sprig**

In a medium-sized bowl, toss apples with lemon juice. Mix in celery and walnuts. In a small bowl, blend mayonnaise and sour cream. Stir into apple mixture. Arrange lettuce in a serving bowl, on a platter or on individual salad plates. Top with apple mixture. Garnish with a sprig of watercress or parsley. Makes 6 to 8 servings.

Amish Orange Salad with Poppy Seeds

An Amish Country inn serves this salad the year round with their skillet-fried chicken. In the winter, oranges are perfect in the salad, sometimes combined with apples and avocados. In the summer, however, strawberries, peaches, raspberries, plums and a combination of melons can be substituted for the oranges.

> **3 seedless oranges, peeled, sliced**
> **Poppy-Seed Dressing, see below**
> **Sliced avocado (optional)**
>
> *Poppy-Seed Dressing:*
> **1 cup honey**
> **1/4 teaspoon salt**
> **1/2 cup cider vinegar**
> **1-1/3 cups vegetable oil**
> **2 teaspoons poppy seeds**

Arrange orange slices on a platter or 4 individual salad plates. Prepare Poppy-Seed Dressing. Garnish salad with avocado slices, if desired. Offer dressing at the table to spoon over individual servings. Makes 4 servings.

To prepare Poppy-Seed Dressing: In a jar with a lid, combine dressing ingredients; shake to blend. Refrigerate until ready to serve. Shake before serving. Makes 2-3/4 cups.

Cranberry-Orange Relish

Cranberries, in any form, could compete with apple pie for being the most "all-American" addition to any menu. This uncooked relish is simple and an old favorite. It was the standard accompaniment to almost all meat and poultry main dishes and also some fish dishes in the early days of New England.

> **4 cups raw cranberries, washed, picked over**
> **2 oranges**
> **1-3/4 cups sugar**

Put cranberries through a food chopper. Peel oranges and remove seeds. Put peel and flesh through chopper. Or, turn cranberries into a food processor fitted with the steel blade. Process with quick on/off pulses until cranberries are finely chopped. Turn into a large bowl. Chop orange peel and flesh in the food processor. Add to cranberries. Add sugar. Stir until blended. Let stand a few hours before serving. Makes about 4 cups.

Zucchini Relish

—— •◆• ——

If you get one zucchini plant to produce, you will most likely have too many zucchini. Occasionally, one will get away and expand like a little whale. That's the one to use for relish!

2-1/2 quarts shredded, deseeded, unpared zucchini
3 cups shredded fresh onions
5 tablespoons salt
2-1/2 cups white or cider vinegar
5 cups sugar
1 tablespoon *each* freshly grated nutmeg, mustard powder,
**   turmeric and cornstarch**
1/8 teaspoon red (cayenne) pepper
1 green bell pepper, chopped
1 red bell pepper, chopped

In a large bowl, combine zucchini and onions. Sprinkle with salt; let stand overnight. The next day, put 6 (1-pint) or 12 (1/2-pint) canning jars with rings and lids into a large pot of water. Bring to a simmer. Drain zucchini and onions. Rinse in cold water; drain. In a large non-aluminum kettle, combine zucchini, onions, vinegar, sugar, spices, cornstarch and bell peppers. Bring to a boil, stirring. Reduce heat and simmer, uncovered, 30 to 40 minutes or until mixture has cooked down and thickened. There should be little "loose" liquid. Spoon into hot sterilized jars. Cap with sterilized lids and rings. Place filled capped jars on a rack in a large canning kettle. Add boiling water until jars are covered with 2 inches of water. Simmer 15 minutes. Remove from water and cool on racks away from drafts. Label before storing. Makes 6 (1-pint) or 12 (1/2-pint) jars.

Homemade Tomato Ketchup

———————————————— • ♦ • ————————————————

This is a hot, Southern-style ketchup. While working with the hot chilies, wear rubber gloves and be careful not to touch your face or eyes. Rinse the chilies clean and break or cut the pods in half. Remove the seeds, then chop. To make the chilies less hot, soak them in cold salted water for 1 hour.

> **4 pounds ripe, firm tomatoes**
> **2 cups finely chopped onions**
> **1-1/2 cups packed light-brown sugar**
> **1-1/2 cups white vinegar**
> **5 tablespoons mixed pickling spices**
> **1 tablespoon finely chopped, fresh, red, hot chili**
> **1-1/2 teaspoons salt**

In a 6-quart, stainless-steel or enamelled pot, combine all ingredients. Bring to a boil over high heat. Stir until sugar dissolves. Reduce heat to low. Simmer 30 to 40 minutes or until mixture is thick enough to hold its shape in a spoon. Stir often to prevent scorching. Turn mixture into a food processor fitted with the steel blade. Process until smooth. Cool and refrigerate. Ketchup keeps about 1 month. If desired, you may pour hot mixture into 4, hot, sterilized, 1/2-pint canning jars. Cap with sterilized lids and rings. Place on a rack in a large canning kettle. Add boiling water until jars are covered with 2 inches of water. Simmer 15 minutes. Remove from water and cool on racks away from drafts. Label before storing. Makes 4 (1/2-pint) jars.

◆ BREADS ◆

One of the greatest contributions made to the American table by the immigrants was the great variety of breads these people introduced. Every country has given us at least one or two. From Scandinavia came knackebrod which we know commercially as Ry-Krisp. Euphrates bread arrived from Asia Minor. The Jewish community introduced the bagel. Rye breads have come from almost every northern European country. The French have given us croissants, buttery rolls and crusty baguettes. Italian bread, similar to French bread, is standard on most restaurant tables, while the familiar sliced white bread can be traced directly back to England.

The hearth is historically the heart of the country American home. From the beginning, baking has been an art. Pioneer women made their own yeast, used whatever kind of flour was available, and baked perfect bread in primitive ovens. Bread and soup were so often the whole meal that the bread had to be good.

In the words of homemakers in colonial days, "When bread rises in the oven, the heart of the housewife rises with it." Bread was con-

sidered vitally important to the nourishment of the family and all early homemakers knew how to make it. Marion Tyree writing in *Housekeeping in Old Virginia*, 1879, advocated the positive approach. She said, "Resolve that you *will* have good bread, and never cease striving after this result till you have effected it."

In the Pennsylvania Dutch home, Friday was considered a lucky day so it became baking day. Friday was also a day *not* to do certain things, like sweep the floor, cultivate plants, sow peas or beans. And, there were other superstitions and rules. For instance, loaves could never be placed upside down on the table or the family would fight. They could not be placed on their sides or the angels would weep. To ward off homesickness, a loaf of bread and a broom had to be sent off to the new home of somebody moving away, and in moving, the dough trough had to be carried into the house before anything else.

I hope the selection of recipes that I have chosen for this section encourages you to research and bake other traditional American breads.

Icebox Yeast Dough

—— • ◆ • ——

Rural American cooks have been excellent bakers throughout the history of our country. So there would always be bread, a chilled yeast dough was kept on hand, especially after the advent of the refrigerator about 50 years ago. From this basic dough many variations are possible. Among them favorite "dinner rolls" called *Parkerhouse rolls*. It was in 1885 that Harvey D. Parker opened a restaurant in Boston based on the notion that patrons would like to eat meals at irregular hours. Up until this time, restaurants only offered food at fixed hours. It was at Mr. Parker's eating house that Parkerhouse rolls were first served.

> 2 (1/4-ounce) packages active dry yeast (scant 2 tablespoons)
> 1 cup warm water (105F to 115F, 40C to 45C)
> 1/2 cup butter, melted
> 1/2 cup sugar
> 3 eggs
> 1 teaspoon salt
> About 4 cups unbleached bread or all-purpose flour

In a large bowl, combine yeast and warm water; stir. Let stand about 5 minutes or until yeast foams. Stir in butter, sugar, eggs and salt. Beat in flour, 1 cup at a time, until dough is too stiff to mix which may be before all of flour is added. Cover and refrigerate 2 hours or up to 4 days. Proceed as directed in 1 of the variations below.

Variations

Parkerhouse Rolls: Cut chilled dough into quarters. On a lightly floured board, roll out 1 part at a time to 1/2 inch thick. Cut into 3-inch rounds. Brush with melted butter. Crease each round of dough just off center. Fold each piece of dough so larger part of fold is on top side of roll. Place on lightly greased baking sheets. Brush with additional melted butter. Cover and let rise until doubled in bulk, about 45 minutes. Preheat oven to 375F (190C). Bake 15 minutes or until golden. Makes 48 rolls.

Giant Caramel-Pecan Rolls: On a lightly floured board, roll out chilled dough to a 12-inch square. Brush with 1/2 cup softened butter. Sprinkle with a mixture of 1/2 cup packed brown sugar and 2 teaspoons ground cinnamon. Roll up jelly-roll fashion. Cut into 12 equal slices. Melt 1/2 cup butter in the bottom of a 13" x 9" baking pan. Sprinkle with 1/2 cup packed brown sugar. Drizzle with 1/2 cup dark corn syrup. Sprinkle with 1 cup chopped pecans. Arrange dough slices evenly over nuts in baking pan. Cover and let rise until almost doubled in bulk, about 1 hour. Preheat oven to 350F (175C). Bake rolls 25 minutes or until golden. Let cool slightly, then turn out of pan while still warm. Makes 12 giant rolls.

Pennsylvania Dutch "Strickle" Sheets: Grease a 17-1/2" x 11-1/2" jelly-roll pan. Pat chilled dough into pan making an even layer. Cover and let rise until puffy, about 45 minutes. Meanwhile, combine 2 cups packed light-brown sugar, 1/4 cup softened butter and 1/4 cup all-purpose flour until crumbly. Mix in 1/4 cup boiling water. Stir until blended. With your fingers, poke holes into risen dough, spacing holes about 2 inches apart. Sprinkle crumbly mixture over top. Preheat oven to 350F (175C). Bake sheets 20 to 25 minutes or until golden. Serve warm. Makes 24 servings.

Cardamom Bread: Add 1 teaspoon freshly crushed cardamom pods and 1/2 cup nonfat dry milk solids to liquid mixture. Divide chilled dough into 2 parts. Divide each part into 3. Shape into 3-foot ropes. Braid 3 ropes together to make each loaf. Place 2 loaves on a greased baking sheet. Cover and let rise until puffy, 45 minutes to 1 hour. Preheat oven to 375F (190C). Brush dough with a mixture of egg and milk. Sprinkle with sliced almonds or pearl sugar. Bake 20 to 25 minutes or until golden. Makes 2 loaves.

Christmas Wreath: Prepare Cardamom Bread, above. Divide chilled dough into 3 parts. Shape into long ropes and make 1 long braid. Shape into a wreath on a greased, large, baking sheet or pizza pan. Let rise and bake as for Cardamom Bread.

Note: When rolling dough into long ropes, it is helpful to work on a lightly oiled countertop. Dust the dough lightly with flour, if necessary.

Anadama Bread

Exasperated by his lazy wife's habit of serving cornmeal mush every day, a Massachussets fisherman is said to have added yeast to the mush to make a loaf of bread. He christened his successful creation in honor of his wife by exclaiming "Anna, damn her."

> 2 cups water
> 1 teaspoon salt
> 1/2 cup yellow cornmeal
> 1/2 cup dark molasses
> 2 tablespoons butter
> 2 (1/4-ounce) packages active dry yeast (scant 2 tablespoons)
> 1/2 cup warm water (105F to 115F, 40C to 45C)
> 4-1/2 to 5 cups unbleached bread or all-purpose flour

Lightly grease 2 baking sheets or 2 round, 9-inch, cake pans. In a medium-sized saucepan, combine 2 cups water, salt and cornmeal. Bring to a boil and cook until thickened, stirring constantly. Remove from heat. Add molasses and butter. Set aside until cooled to lukewarm. In a large bowl, combine yeast and warm water; stir. Let stand about 5 minutes or until yeast foams. Add cooled cornmeal mixture. Stir in half of flour; beat well. Gradually stir in enough of remaining flour to make a stiff dough. Turn out onto a lightly floured board. Knead until smooth and springy, about 10 minutes. Wash and oil bowl. Place dough in bowl, turning to oil all sides. Cover and let rise in a warm place until doubled in bulk, 1 to 1-1/2 hours. Punch down dough. Turn out onto board. Knead 30 seconds to squeeze out air bubbles. Divide dough into 2 parts and shape into 2 round loaves. Place on greased baking sheets or in greased cake pans. Cover and let rise until almost doubled, 45 minutes to 1 hour. Preheat oven to 375F (190C). Bake 40 to 45 minutes or until a wooden skewer inserted in bread comes out smoothly. Remove from pans. Cool on racks. Makes 2 loaves.

Country-Hearth Bread

·◆·

The Minneapolis Grain Exchange was established in 1887. At that time Minneapolis became the capital of the nation's flour industry. In the late 1800's a "middlings purifier" was invented which removed the bran from spring wheat and produced a superior white flour. This established Minnesota flour as being the finest in the country.

> **1 (1/4-ounce) package active dry yeast (about 1 tablespoon)**
> **2 teaspoons sugar**
> **1/4 cup warm water (105F to 115F, 40C to 45C)**
> **1 pint milk (2 cups)**
> **1 teaspoon salt**
> **2 tablespoons lard, butter or shortening, melted**
> **5 to 5-1/2 cups unbleached bread or all-purpose flour**
> **Milk**

Grease a baking sheet or 2 (9" x 5") loaf pans. In a large bowl, combine yeast, sugar and warm water; stir. Let stand about 5 minutes or until yeast foams. Scald milk by heating almost to boiling point. Cool to 105F to 115F (40C to 45C) or until a few drops on your wrist feel warm. Add salt, warm milk and melted fat to yeast mixture. Beat in 2 cups flour, beating until smooth. Add enough of remaining flour, a little at a time, until a stiff dough forms. Cover bowl and let rest 15 minutes. Turn out dough onto a lightly floured board. Knead, adding flour sparingly until dough is smooth and springy, about 10 minutes. Wash and oil bowl. Place dough in bowl, turning to oil all sides. Cover and let rise in a warm place until doubled in bulk, 1 to 1-1/2 hours. Punch down dough. Turn out onto board. Knead 30 seconds to squeeze out air bubbles. Shape into 1 large round loaf. Place on greased baking sheet. Or, divide dough into 2 parts and shape into 2 oblong loaves. Fit into greased loaf pans, smooth-side up. Cover and let rise until almost doubled, 45 minutes to 1 hour. Brush tops of loaves with milk; sprinkle with flour. Preheat oven to 375F (190C). Bake 25 to 35 minutes or until a wooden skewer inserted in bread comes out smoothly. Remove from pans. Cool on racks. Makes 1 round or 2 oblong loaves.

Variations
Swedish Rye Bread: Add 1 tablespoon *each* caraway seed, anise seed and fennel seed to flour. Mix in grated peel of 1 orange. Substitute 2 cups rye flour for 2 cups all-purpose flour. Substitute 1/3 cup packed brown sugar or molasses for granulated sugar. Mix and let rise as above. Shape into 2 round loaves. Place dough, smooth-side up, in 2 greased, round, 9-inch cake pans. Let rise and bake as above.

Honey Whole-Wheat Bread: Substitute 2 cups whole-wheat flour for 2 cups white flour. Substitute 2 tablespoons honey for sugar. Replace 1/2 cup milk with 2 eggs. Add 1/4 cup melted lard to dough instead of 2 tablespoons fat. Mix and let rise as above. Shape into 2 loaves. Place dough in 2 greased (9" x 5") loaf pans. Let rise and bake as above.

Oatmeal Bread: Substitute 1/2 cup light molasses for sugar and 2 cups uncooked rolled oats for 1 cup flour. Mix and let rise as above. Shape into 2 round loaves. Place dough, smooth-side up, in 2 greased, round, 9-inch cake pans. Let rise and bake as above.

Buttermilk Pancakes or Waffles

— ◆ —

As one of the earliest forms of baking, pancakes were once called *hearth cakes*. The Dutch settlers brought both pancakes and their "waffre" irons to America. The original irons had long handles so the waffles could be baked over an open fire. Pancakes and waffles were served not only for breakfast, but for supper and noon meals.

> **2 eggs**
> **1/2 pint buttermilk (1 cup)**
> **1/2 teaspoon baking soda**
> **1-1/4 cups all-purpose flour**
> **1 tablespoon sugar**
> **1 teaspoon baking powder**
> **1/2 teaspoon salt**
> **2 tablespoons melted vegetable shortening or vegetable oil**
> **Butter or fat**

If making pancakes, heat a heavy griddle slowly while mixing batter. In a large bowl, beat eggs. In a small bowl, mix buttermilk and baking soda. Add to eggs. In a medium-sized bowl, combine flour, sugar, baking powder and salt. Stir into egg mixture. Blend in shortening or oil.

For pancakes: Heat griddle until drops of water dance on it. Brush with butter or fat. Spoon 1/4 cup batter for each cake onto hot griddle. Cook until golden on each side. Makes 16 (4-inch) pancakes.

For waffles: Heat waffle iron. Spoon batter into heated waffle iron. Close iron. Bake until golden. Makes 8 (6- to 8-inch) waffles.

Variations

Blueberry Pancakes: Add 1/2 to 1 cup fresh or frozen blueberries to batter just before cooking pancakes. Cook as above.

Sweet-Milk Pancakes or Waffles: Substitute fresh milk for buttermilk. Omit baking soda and use an additional 1/2 teaspoon baking powder. For lighter pancakes, separate eggs and make batter using yolks. Beat egg whites until stiff; fold into batter. Cook as above.

Southern Corn Cakes: In place of all-purpose flour, use a combination of 3/4 cup cornmeal and 1/4 cup all-purpose flour. Cook as above.

Swedish Pancakes: Substitute fresh milk for buttermilk. Omit baking soda and reduce flour to 1/2 cup. Cook as above. Pancakes will be thin and lacy. Fill with berries and whipped cream.

Coconut Waffles: Add 1 cup flaked coconut to batter. Cook as above. Serve with coconut syrup and whipped cream.

Pecan Waffles: Spoon batter into a heated waffle iron. Sprinkle with chopped pecans. Close iron. Bake until golden.

Note: Coconut syrup is often used in mixed drinks and can be found in the beverage section of supermarkets. It makes an excellent topping for waffles and pancakes.

Funnel Cakes

◆

Originally a Dutch classic but adopted by many countries, batter drizzled into hot fat is called *tippaleipa* in Finnish. A pastry bag with a large tip is easier to handle than putting the batter through a funnel.

Fat
3 eggs
1/4 cup granulated sugar
1 pint milk (2 cups)
3/4 cup all-purpose flour
1/2 teaspoon salt
2 teaspoons baking powder
Powdered sugar

In a deep-fat fryer or deep heavy skillet, begin heating fat to 375F (190C) or until a 1-inch cube of bread turns golden brown in 50 seconds. In a large bowl, beat eggs, granulated sugar and milk. Sift in flour, salt and baking powder. Beat until smooth. Batter should be thin. Pour through a funnel and drizzle into hot fat, using your finger to stop batter as necessary. Or, put batter into a large pastry bag fitted with a 1/4- to 1/2-inch tip. Squeeze batter into hot fat. Swirl batter around as you drizzle it into fat. Fry cakes 2 to 3 minutes or until golden, turning once. Using a slotted spoon, remove from fat and drain on paper towels. Sift powdered sugar over top of cakes and serve immediately. Makes about 12 large cakes.

Honey-Maple-Cinnamon Syrup

◆

A lovely syrup for your pancakes or waffles.

1 cup honey
1/2 cup maple syrup
1 teaspoon ground cinnamon

In a small saucepan, combine all ingredients. Heat gently until blended. Drizzle over hot pancakes or waffles. Makes 1-1/2 cups.

Oylykoeks, Fastnachts or Doughnuts

—— • ◆ • ——

A political historian might consider the role of the Dutch on American politics relatively small, but remember that the Dutch gave us doughnuts. One might conclude that the Dutch exert their influence on our political campaigns at the all-important coffeepot!

Not only have the Pennsylvania Dutch always been adept at making doughnuts, but so too were the Dutch who lived in the northern part of New England. They would make doughnuts spiced with molasses which were cut and twisted in strips about 1 inch wide by 4 inches long. Pinched together and fried in deep fat they made golden rings, light, crisp and delicious. This basic recipe is a classic for yeast-raised doughnuts.

> 1/2 pint milk (1 cup)
> 1 (1/4-ounce) package active dry yeast (about 1 tablespoon)
> 3-1/2 cups all-purpose flour
> 1/4 cup vegetable shortening
> 1 teaspoon salt
> 1/4 cup sugar
> 1 egg
> Fat
> Additional sugar

Scald milk by heating almost to boiling point. Pour into a large bowl. Cool to 105F to 115F (40C to 45C) or until a few drops on your wrist feel warm. Sprinkle yeast over milk. Let stand until yeast foams. Add half of flour; beat until smooth. Cover and let rise 2 hours in a warm place. In another bowl, beat shortening, salt and 1/4 cup sugar until blended and light. Add egg; mix well. Stir into yeast mixture along with remaining flour. Beat 5 minutes with a wooden spoon. Cover and let rise again in a warm place until doubled in bulk, 45 minutes to 1 hour. Turn out onto a lightly oiled surface. Roll out to 1/2 to 3/4 inch thick. With a floured cutter, cut out doughnuts. Let rise until doubled, about 45 minutes. Meanwhile, in a deep-fat fryer or deep heavy skillet, heat fat to 365F to 375F (185C to 190C) or until a 1-inch cube of bread turns golden brown in 50 seconds. Fry doughnuts 3 to 5 minutes or until golden, turning them once. Using a slotted spoon, remove from fat and drain on paper towels. Sprinkle with sugar. Makes 24 (3-inch) doughnuts.

Sopaipillas

These resemble "sofa pillows" and are fried like donuts but have hollow centers. Some people serve sopaipillas with butter and honey, mesquite honey if possible. There are two varieties. One is made with unsweetened yeast dough, rolled out like biscuits, cut into squares and deep-fried. The other is made like baking-powder biscuits and deep-fried. They're always served fresh from the frying kettle. They may be served with a meal or dusted with powdered sugar and served with coffee or hot chocolate.

1-1/2 cups all-purpose flour
1/4 teaspoon salt
1-1/2 teaspoons baking powder
2 tablespoons lard
1 egg
Water
Hot fat

In a large bowl, sift together flour, salt and baking powder. Using a pastry blender or 2 knives, cut in lard until mixture resembles crumbs. Add egg and just enough water to make a stiff dough. On a lightly floured surface, roll out dough very thin. Cut into diamond shapes or squares about 2 inches in diameter. In a deep-fat fryer or deep heavy skillet, fat to 400C to 425F (205C to 215C) or until a 1-inch cube of bread turns golden brown in 15 seconds. Fry diamonds or squares until puffed and golden, turning once to brown both sides. With a slotted spoon, remove from fat; drain on paper towels. Serve immediately for breakfast or lunch or as an accompaniment to barbecued steaks. Makes 12 sopaipillas.

Beaten Biscuits

—— • ♦ • ——

If it were not for the kitchen slaves of the old South, this delicious hot bread would not exist at all. To achieve just the right texture and lightness the dough must be beaten hard. If the biscuits are intended for everyday eating, 300 to 500 whacks are enough, but for the very best biscuits they had to be beaten for nearly an hour! To do it, the dough was placed on the surface of a tree stump and beaten with an iron pestle or side of a hatchet or axe until the dough had little blisters of air and was smooth and satiny.

Our modern kitchen wizards, the food processor or the heavy-duty mixer make the job of "beating the biscuits" simple for today's baker! I give three methods of mixing below: the food processor, heavy-duty mixer and the old-fashioned hand method.

Beaten Biscuits make great bases for canapés. The cup-like halves will hold tiny bits of creamed and salad-style fillings.

> **2 cups all-purpose flour**
> **1/2 teaspoon salt**
> **3 tablespoons lard, butter or vegetable shortening**
> **1 egg**
> **1/2 cup cold milk**

Preheat oven to 350F (175C).

To mix in a food processor: Fit food processor with the steel blade. Add flour, salt and lard, butter or shortening to the work bowl. Process until fat is worked into dry ingredients. In a small bowl, mix egg and milk. Pour liquid through feed tube with processor on until a ball of dough forms that spins around work bowl. Process 3 minutes longer.

To mix using a heavy-duty mixer: Combine flour, salt and lard, butter or shortening in the mixing bowl. Attach the dough paddle (not dough hook) to mixer. Turn on mixer and mix until fat is blended into dry ingredients. Add egg and milk and turn on mixer. Mix 25 minutes or until dough blisters and is very satiny.

To mix by hand: In a large bowl, mix flour with salt. Using a pastry blender or 2 knives, cut in lard, butter or shortening until completely blended. In a small bowl, mix egg and milk. Stir into flour mixture to make a stiff dough. Put dough on a block or countertop. Beat with a blunt wooden mallet until dough blisters; this takes about 25 minutes. Fold edges of dough toward center as you beat it.

To roll, cut-out and bake: On a lightly oiled surface, roll out dough to a 14-inch square. Fold dough in half and press layers together. Roll out again to same size to smooth out edges. Cut into 1-1/2-inch rounds. Place on ungreased baking sheets. Pierce each biscuit once with a fork. Bake 25 minutes or until puffed and lightly browned. Remove from oven and split biscuits. If centers are soft, return to oven 3 to 4 minutes longer. Makes about 48 split biscuits.

Old-Fashioned Buttermilk Biscuits

Southerners like buttermilk biscuits served with sausage and grits for breakfast or with fried chicken for any meal.

 2 cups all-purpose flour
 1/2 teaspoon salt
 2 teaspoons baking powder
 1/2 teaspoon baking soda
 1/3 cup lard or vegetable shortening
 1/2 to 2/3 cup buttermilk

Preheat oven to 450F (230C). Sift flour, salt, baking powder and baking soda into a medium-sized bowl. Using a pastry blender or 2 knives, cut in lard or shortening until mixture resembles coarse crumbs. Add buttermilk. Stir just until moistened; do not overmix. Turn out batter onto a floured board; knead very lightly, just until dough is smooth. Roll out to 1/2 inch thick. Cut into 2-inch rounds. Place on ungreased baking sheets. Bake 12 to 15 minutes or until golden. Serve hot. Makes 24 biscuits.

Variations

Southern-Style Biscuits: Use lard. Cut biscuits into 3-inch rounds. Place on ungreased baking sheets 1/2 inch apart. Dust tops of biscuits with flour. Bake as above.
Calico Biscuits: Add 1/2 cup finely chopped green bell pepper, 3 tablespoons finely chopped drained pimientos and 2 tablespoons minced fresh onion to flour mixture before adding buttermilk. Bake as above.
Ranch-Style Biscuits: Divide dough into 4 parts. Pat into circles about 3/4 inch thick. Bake as above. Makes 4 large biscuits.
Whole-Wheat Biscuits: Substitute whole-wheat flour for all-purpose flour. Bake as above.
Baking-Powder Biscuits: Use 3 teaspoons baking powder and omit baking soda. Replace buttermilk with fresh milk. Bake as above.
Cornmeal Biscuits: Add 1/2 cup cornmeal and 3 tablespoons sugar to flour mixture. Bake as above.

Cornmeal Spoon Bread

◆

This is called *spoon bread* because it is spooned from the pan. Often served for breakfast, it is delicious with butter and maple syrup. Some like it with the main course at dinner in place of bread or potatoes. In Virginia, it is a tradition to serve spoon bread with fried tomatoes.

>1 cup boiling water
>1/2 cup cornmeal
>1/2 cup milk
>1/2 cup all-purpose flour
>1-1/2 teaspoons baking powder
>1/2 teaspoon salt
>1 tablespoon softened or melted butter
>4 eggs, separated

Preheat oven to 400F (205C). Grease a 1-quart casserole or soufflé dish. Pour boiling water over cornmeal in a medium-sized bowl. Beat in milk. In a small bowl, mix flour, baking powder and salt. Stir into cornmeal mixture with butter and egg yolks. In a large bowl, beat egg whites until stiff; fold into cornmeal mixture. Turn into greased dish. Bake just until puffed and golden, 25 to 30 minutes; do not overbake. Serve immediately. Makes 4 to 6 servings.

Early American Corn Breads

Hoe cake and *corn pone* were the first basic forms of corn bread baked in the South. They were simply cornmeal mixed with water, salted and baked. Hoe cake was baked on the flat side of a cotton hoe over hot embers. Pones were the "appones" of the Indians, shaped with the hands into small cakes and baked over an open fire. Spoon bread and batter bread evolved when old-time Southern cooks put a dish of cornmeal mush into the oven.

Johnnycake

Johnnycake, the cornmeal bread that colonists first called *journey cake,* is one that seems to originate from a large area of the eastern part of our country. Some say the first name originated from trips into the wilderness during which corn bread was cooked by campfires along the way. In Rhode Island, it is spelled without the "h" and it is made with white cornmeal. The first colonists learned from the Indians to make the cakes and called them *Shawnee cakes.* They're also known as *hoe cakes, ash cakes,* and *corn pone.* Each is cooked in a different way and each has its own special quality. The best cakes are made from the hard variety of corn which grows in the North. Many Southern corn breads call for "dent" corn so named for the dents in the dry kernel.

> **1 cup stone-ground cornmeal**
> **1 teaspoon sugar**
> **1/4 teaspoon salt**
> **1-1/4 cups boiling water**
> **1 tablespoon butter, melted**
> **Bacon drippings**
> **Butter**
> **Maple syrup**

In a medium-sized bowl, combine cornmeal, sugar and salt. Add boiling water and melted butter; stir until smooth. Place a 10-inch skillet over medium-high heat. Brush with bacon drippings. Drop batter by tablespoonfuls onto hot skillet, making a few cakes at a time. Cook until crisp and browned on 1 side. Turn and cook until underside is golden. Repeat with remaining batter, brushing skillet with more bacon drippings as required. Serve hot with butter and maple syrup. Makes about 24 cakes.

Northern Johnnycake or Corn Bread

While the Southern-style Johnnycake was basically a cooked cornmeal mixture baked on a griddle into pancakes, the Northern variety is more like a baked corn bread.

> **1-1/2 cups all-purpose flour**
> **1-1/2 cups stone-ground cornmeal**
> **1/2 cup sugar**
> **1 teaspoon salt**
> **1 teaspoon baking soda**
> **1/2 pint buttermilk (1 cup)**
> **3/4 cup vegetable oil**
> **2 eggs**

Preheat oven to 375F (190C). Lightly grease a 13" x 9" baking pan. In a large bowl, stir together flour, cornmeal, sugar, salt and baking soda. Add buttermilk, oil and eggs. Stir just until blended; do not overmix. Pour mixture into greased baking pan. Bake 25 to 30 minutes or just until cake springs back when touched in center. Makes 12 servings.

Hopi Indian Blue Cornmeal Cakes

— ◆ —

Blue cornmeal has historically been used by the Indians of the Southwest. The colorful corn has a deep-blue layer of bran which when ground produces a grayish-blue meal. Cooked into a cereal, using one-third cup meal to one cup water, it turns into a pale pinkish porridge which is delicious served with just a dab of butter.

You may substitute blue cornmeal for stone-ground cornmeal in any recipe. Try these griddle cakes served with real Northern maple syrup!

3/4 cup blue cornmeal
3/4 cup all-purpose flour
2 teaspoons baking powder
2 teaspoons vegetable oil
1/2 teaspoon salt
1 to 1-1/2 cups milk
Butter or fat
Maple syrup or fresh fruit

In a medium-sized bowl, combine cornmeal, flour, baking powder, oil and salt. Add milk to give the consistency you prefer for griddlecakes; for thicker cakes, use 1 cup, for thinner cakes, use 1-1/2 cups. Stir just until lumps disappear; do not overmix. Heat griddle over medium-high heat until drops of water dance on it. Brush with butter or fat. Drop batter onto hot griddle, using 1/4 cup batter for each cake. Cook each cake until crisp on 1 side. With a pancake turner, turn and cook until underside is golden. Brush griddle with more fat as required. Serve hot with butter and maple syrup or fresh fruit. Makes 8 to 10 cakes.

Hush Puppies

— ◆ —

"Y'all want some hosh poppies?" This invitation by a waitress to order a food about which I knew nothing, piqued my curiousity. As a Northerner, I wasn't quite sure what she meant. This was in the days before every food magazine and cookbook included recipes for regional, rather earthy, foods. Why the name "hush puppies"? An old Southern legend explains the name of these fried breads. It seems that the dogs that went along on hunting expeditions, being a hungry lot, would start yelping as soon as they caught the smell of fish frying for their masters' dinner. To appease them, the hunters dropped bits of cornmeal batter into the fish pan and tossed the fried cakes to the dogs with the gentle rebuke, "Hush puppy!"

> **Fat**
> **1-1/2 cups stone-ground cornmeal**
> **1/2 cup all-purpose flour**
> **2 teaspoons baking powder**
> **1/2 teaspoon salt**
> **1 egg**
> **3/4 cup milk**
> **1 small onion, grated**

In a deep heavy skillet, heat fat to 375F (190C) or until a 1-inch cube of bread turns golden brown in 50 seconds. In a large bowl, combine cornmeal, flour, baking powder and salt. In a small bowl, mix egg, milk and onion. Add to cornmeal mixture. Drop batter from a spoon into hot fat. Fry about 1 minute or until crisp and golden. Using a slotted spoon, remove from fat and drain on paper towels. Serve hot. Makes about 20.

Popovers

•◆•

It isn't surprising that popovers are a favorite American quick bread. The English bake the same batter along with a roast of beef and call it *Yorkshire pudding*. The Dutch bake it in a large shallow pan and call it *Dutch babies* and serve it for breakfast, as do the Finns, Swedes, Norwegians and Germans who simply know it as an *oven pancake*.

Baked in individual tins, the American-invented muffin pan, the mixture "pops over" the top of the pan making a high, hollow-centered, crisp, crusted bread. In order to pop properly, the pans must be filled full enough to allow enough batter for the top. Fill them to about 1/4 inch from the top of each cup. This recipe will make nine popovers in muffin tins with one-third-cup capacity, or six in tins that hold half a cup.

> 1 cup all-purpose flour
> 1/2 teaspoon salt
> 2 eggs
> 1 cup milk
> 1 tablespoon vegetable oil

Preheat oven to 425F (220C). Generously grease 6 or 9 muffin tins. In a medium-sized bowl, stir together all ingredients. Pour into greased muffin tins to within 1/4 inch of top of each cup. Bake 35 minutes or until popped and golden. Pierce side of each popover, if desired, and return to turned-off oven 10 to 15 minutes to dry. Makes 6 servings.

Flour Tortillas

•◆•

Wheat-based tortillas are favorites with many Americans and were first made in the Southwest. Although they are most often purchased in the grocery, they can be made at home.

> 3 cups all-purpose flour
> 1-1/2 teaspoons salt
> 1/4 cup lard
> Tepid water

Measure flour and salt into a large bowl, or into the workbowl of a food processor with the steel blade in place. Using a pastry blender or 2 knives, cut in lard until mixture resembles coarse crumbs. Or, cut in using food processor. With processor on, or stirring with a fork, add enough tepid water to make a stiff smooth dough. On a lightly floured board, knead until dough forms a smooth ball. Cover and let stand 15 minutes. Divide into 12 parts. Roll out dough, 1 part at a time, to thin rounds about 10 inches in diameter. Heat a heavy skillet or griddle over medium-high heat until drops of water dance on it. Cook tortillas, 1 at a time, about 1-1/2 minutes on each side or until brown spots appear, but tortillas are still flexible. Stack them as they are cooked. Serve immediately. Or, cool and wrap airtight and store in refrigerator. Tortillas can also be stored well-wrapped in the freezer up to 3 months. Makes 12 tortillas.

Country-Style Muffins

———————————— •♦• ————————————

Muffins originated in England and were a yeast-raised "tea cake." American-style muffins are a quick bread leavened with baking powder and/or baking soda. They often include fruit and nuts. We serve them mainly for breakfast. The name "muffin" is believed to have come from a German word *muffe* for cake. Today, muffins range in size from miniatures to giant ones that could serve three persons.

> 2 cups all-purpose flour
> 1/3 cup sugar
> 1 tablespoon baking powder
> 1/2 teaspoon salt
> 1/3 cup softened butter or vegetable shortening
> 1 egg
> 1 cup milk

Preheat oven to 400F (205C). Grease 12 medium-sized muffin cups or line with cupcake liners. In a large bowl, combine flour, sugar, baking powder and salt. Add butter or shortening, egg and milk. Stir with a fork just until ingredients are blended. Fill prepared muffin cups two-thirds full. Bake 20 to 25 minutes or until golden and a wooden pick inserted in center of a muffin comes out clean. Serve hot with butter, jam, marmalade, honey or other favorite spread. Makes 12 muffins.

Variations
Whole-Wheat Muffins: Substitute 1 cup whole-wheat flour for 1 cup all-purpose flour. Use only 2 teaspoons baking powder. Bake as above.
Sour-Cream Muffins: Use only 2 teaspoons baking powder and add 1/2 teaspoon baking soda. Substitute dairy sour cream for milk. Bake as above.
Blueberry Muffins: Add additional 2 tablespoons sugar. When all ingredients are blended, carefully fold in 1 cup fresh or partially thawed frozen blueberries. Bake as above.
Honey-Orange Muffins: Use 2 eggs. Place in bottom of each muffin cup, 1 teaspoon honey and 1 thin slice unpeeled orange cut into quarters. Spoon batter on top. Bake as above.
Apple Muffins: Use 1/2 cup sugar. Add 1/2 teaspoon ground cinnamon to flour mixture. Add 1 cup shredded, raw, tart apple along with butter or shortening. Sprinkle top of batter in cups with a mixture of 1/3 cup packed brown sugar, 1/3 cup chopped walnuts and 1/2 teaspoon ground cinnamon. Bake as above.
Date & Nut Muffins: Add 1 cup *each* finely chopped dates and finely chopped walnuts or pecans to flour mixture before adding liquid. Bake as above.

Colonial Brown-Bread Muffins

•◆•

This batter can also be baked in a 9 inch by 5 inch loaf pan for 1 hour until it is done. Very quick and easy!

1 pint buttermilk (2 cups)
2 cups whole-wheat flour
2/3 cup all-purpose flour
1 cup packed brown sugar
2 teaspoons baking soda
1 teaspoon pumpkin-pie spice
1/2 teaspoon salt
3/4 cup light or dark raisins

Preheat oven to 350F (175C). Grease 12 large muffin cups or line with cupcake liners. In a large bowl, combine all ingredients until blended. Fill prepared muffin cups two-thirds full. Bake 25 to 30 minutes or until a wooden pick inserted in center of a muffin comes out clean. Makes 12 muffins.

Boston Brown Bread

·◆·

Boston brown bread was steamed on top of the range while baked beans simmered in brick ovens. The hot, molasses-flavored loaves, commonly made with cornmeal, rye, white and graham flours and often with raisins added, held a time-honored place on Saturday's bread tray. They were to be cut into thick slices while still hot and slathered with butter. Another name for the bread is "Ryaninjun." In old cookbooks, cornmeal was often referred to as "Indian meal."

> **2 cups stone-ground cornmeal**
> **1 cup *each* whole-wheat flour, rye flour and all-purpose flour**
> **2 teaspoons baking soda**
> **1 teaspoon salt**
> **1 cup molasses**
> **1 pint buttermilk (2 cups)**
> **1-1/2 cups milk**
> **1 cup raisins**

Fit a deep kettle (one designed for canning is ideal), with a rack. Generously grease 8 to 10 (12- to 16-ounce) metal cans. Cut and butter 8 to 10 squares of foil to fit over tops of cans. In a large bowl, combine all ingredients. Stir until blended. Turn into greased cans, filling them two-thirds full. Top with buttered squares of foil; fasten with string. Place in kettle on rack. Add boiling water to come halfway up sides of cans. Simmer 2-1/2 hours, adding water as necessary. Remove breads from steamer. Cool on racks 10 minutes. Turn out of cans. Serve warm with butter. Makes 8 to 10 loaves.

White Nut Loaf

Bake sales are regular events during autumn in the country. Nut loaves and muffins, yeast breads and coffeecakes on display rival the homiest of window arrangements in a city bakery. At a country bake sale, everybody knows what everybody else contributes so each baker contributes only the finest she can produce!

3/4 cup sugar
3 tablespoons softened butter or vegetable shortening
1 egg
1-1/2 cups milk
2-3/4 cups all-purpose flour
1 tablespoon baking powder
1/2 teaspoon salt
1 cup chopped walnuts, pecans or filberts

Preheat oven to 350F (175C). Grease a 9" x 5" loaf pan. In a large bowl, mix sugar, butter or shortening, egg and milk until blended. Sift flour, baking powder and salt into a medium-sized bowl. Stir into egg mixture just until dry ingredients are moistened; do not overmix. Fold in nuts. Pour into greased pan. Bake 55 to 60 minutes or until a wooden skewer inserted in center comes out clean. Remove from pan; cool on a rack. Makes 1 loaf.

Variations
Fig- or Date-Nut Loaf: Add 3/4 cup chopped figs or dates to batter along with nuts. Bake as above.
Whole-Wheat Nut Loaf: Substitute 2 cups whole-wheat flour for 2 cups all-purpose flour. Add 1/2 cup chopped dates, if desired, to batter along with nuts. Bake as above.

Dark Fruit-Nut Loaf

—— ◆ ——

A country favorite, the variations provide a way to use up overripe bananas and also give you a quick date-nut loaf which is ideal for holiday entertaining, too.

> 2/3 cup sugar
> 1/3 cup softened butter or vegetable shortening
> 2 eggs
> 3 tablespoons buttermilk
> 1 cup freshly grated apple
> 2 cups all-purpose flour
> 1 teaspoon baking powder
> 1/2 teaspoon baking soda
> 1/2 teaspoon salt
> 1 cup chopped walnuts or pecans

Preheat oven to 350F (175C). Grease a 9" x 5" loaf pan. In a large bowl, beat sugar, butter or shortening and eggs until smooth and light. Stir in buttermilk and grated apple. Sift flour, baking powder, baking soda and salt into a medium-sized bowl. Stir into egg mixture just until ingredients are blended; do not overmix. Fold in nuts. Pour into greased pan. Bake 50 to 60 minutes or until a wooden skewer inserted in center comes out clean. Remove from pan; cool on a rack. Makes 1 loaf.

Variations

Banana-Nut Bread: Substitute 1 cup mashed bananas for grated apple. Bake as above.

Date-Nut Bread: Substitute 1/2 cup packed brown sugar for 2/3 cup granulated sugar. Use 1 egg. Omit buttermilk and grated apple. Pour 1 cup boiling water over 1 cup chopped dates; let cool. Add to batter in place of apple. Bake as above.

Orange-Date Loaf: Omit buttermilk and grated apple. Add grated peel of 1 orange. Measure juice from the orange. Add water to equal 1 cup. Add to batter in place of apple. Add 1 cup chopped dates. Bake as above.

Cinnamon-Nut Sour-Cream Coffeecake

—•◆•—

Quick-to-mix coffeecakes are country favorites. They may be baked in a fancy Bundt pan or in an oblong 13 inch by 9 inch baking pan.

> **1 cup butter, softened**
> **1 cup granulated sugar**
> **2 eggs**
> **1/2 pint dairy sour cream (1 cup)**
> **2 cups all-purpose flour**
> **1-1/2 teaspoons baking powder**
> **1/2 teaspoon baking soda**
> **1 teaspoon vanilla extract**
> **3/4 cup chopped walnuts or pecans**
> **1 teaspoon ground cinnamon**
> **2 tablespoons brown sugar**

Preheat oven to 350F (175C). Generously grease and flour either a 13" x 9" baking pan or a 10-inch Bundt pan. In a large bowl, beat butter and granulated sugar until smooth and light. Add eggs. Beat until light. Blend in sour cream. Sift flour, baking powder and baking soda into a medium-sized bowl. Stir into egg mixture along with vanilla. Spoon half of batter into prepared pan. In a small bowl, mix nuts, cinnamon and brown sugar. Sprinkle half of nut mixture onto batter in pan. Top with second half of batter. Sprinkle with remaining nut mixture. Bake 45 to 55 minutes or until a wooden skewer inserted in center comes out clean. Cool on a rack 5 minutes. Turn out of pan. Serve warm. Makes 10 to 12 servings.

Variations

Pennsylvania Dutch Streusel Coffeecake: In place of nut mixture, blend together 1 cup packed brown sugar, 1/4 cup all-purpose flour, 2 tablespoons ground cinnamon, 1/4 cup melted butter and 1 cup chopped walnuts or pecans. Use in the same way as nut mixture. Bake as above.

Blueberry Buckle: Omit nut mixture. Turn entire batter into a greased 13" x 9" baking pan. Sprinkle with 2 cups fresh or unthawed frozen blueberries. Combine 3/4 cup sugar, 1/2 cup all-purpose flour, 1/2 teaspoon ground cinnamon and 1/3 cup softened butter. Sprinkle over blueberries before baking. Bake as above.

Pineapple Coffeecake: Omit nut mixture. Turn entire batter into a greased 13" x 9" baking pan. Spread top of batter with a mixture of 1/2 cup softened butter, 1/2 cup honey and 1 cup well-drained crushed pineapple.

Scandinavian Hardtack

— • ◆ • —

Scandinavians settling in the "new land" brought with them a skill for rolling crisp-bread dough to delicate thinness using hand-carved, hob-nailed rolling pins. Hardtack is a holiday favorite and is made in great quantities to be eaten with gjetost, nokkelost, Jarlsberg and other favorite Scandinavian cheeses.

> **1/2 cup vegetable shortening**
> **1/4 cup butter, softened**
> **3 cups all-purpose flour**
> **2 cups quick-cooking rolled oats**
> **1/2 cup sugar**
> **1-1/2 teaspoons salt**
> **1 teaspoon baking soda**
> **1-1/2 cups buttermilk**

Preheat oven to 325F (165C). In a large bowl, beat shortening and butter until blended. Blend in flour, oats, sugar, salt and baking soda. Stir in buttermilk. Mix until dough is evenly blended. Knead dough into a smooth ball. Wrap in plastic wrap. Refrigerate 30 minutes to 1 hour. Divide into quarters. Lightly dust a board and dough. Working with a quarter of the dough at a time, roll out dough first with a plain rolling pin to about 1/4 inch thick. With a hob-nailed rolling pin, roll out as thin as possible. Cut into 3-inch squares. Transfer squares onto a baking sheet. If you do not use a hob-nailed rolling pin, roll as thin as possible with plain pin but prick squares all over with a fork to make an overall texture. Bake 15 to 18 minutes or until golden and completely dry. Makes 48 (3-inch-square) crisp breads.

◆ CAKES & COOKIES ◆

The earliest recorded recipe for an American cake was published by Amelia Simmons in 1796 in her book, *American Cookery*, where she gave instructions for a soft gingerbread cake. It was in fact almost identical to the standard gingerbread recipe.

Abe Lincoln often quoted a childhood friend who said "Abe, I don't s'pose anybody on earth likes gingerbread better'n I do—and gets less'n I do." Gingerbread and molasses-sweetened puddings date back to Colonial times when sugar was expensive. In addition to molasses, early sweeteners were honey and maple syrup. The Indians extracted sweetening from the cornstalk which they would chew up in small bits, sucking out the sweet juice. In 1650, cane sugar and molasses were imported from the West Indies. It wasn't until 20 years after the assassination of Lincoln that the molasses pitcher was replaced by the sugar bowl on the everyday table. New methods of refining sugar cane had brought the price down to the affordable.

Early cakes were not light and fluffy. Lighter cakes were not developed until granulated sugar became commonly available and baking powder, baking soda and regulated ovens were customary.

Baking pans and tins which we consider standard, are really American inventions. The first loaf pan was used for bread and cake. Loaf cakes were hard to distinguish from what we would call a *quick bread* today. Round, 8- and 9-inch layer pans, 8- and 9-inch square pans, the commonly used 13" x 9" pan and tube-type pans for sponge cake and angel food are all American innovations.

Cookies have developed an American identity, too. The European counterparts are richer, sweeter and fancier than the drop, bar, refrigerator and cut-out cookies we enjoy.

Confections have always been favorites and make welcome gifts around holiday time. They are normally easy enough for a child to make with supervision but can be enjoyed by recipients of all ages.

Jelly Roll

The jelly roll is basically a sponge cake with a jelly filling and has been around since the mid 1800s as a quick, relatively inexpensive dessert. Sometimes the cake was known as a *sponge roll* and sometimes as a *jelly cake*. The roll can be filled with a pudding-type filling such as chocolate or lemon.

> **3/4 cup cake flour**
> **1 teaspoon baking powder**
> **3/4 cup granulated sugar**
> **4 eggs**
> **1/4 teaspoon salt**
> **1/2 teaspoon cream of tartar**
> **1 teaspoon vanilla extract**
> **Powdered sugar**
> **About 2 cups strawberry, red-currant or raspberry jelly or jam**

Preheat oven to 375F (190C). Grease a 15" x 10" jelly-roll pan. Line bottom of pan with parchment or waxed paper. Sift cake flour, baking powder and 1/4 cup granulated sugar together into a medium-sized bowl. In a large bowl, combine eggs, salt, cream of tartar and vanilla. Beat at high speed 5 minutes or by hand until mixture is very fluffy and pale yellow. Add remaining 1/2 cup granulated sugar, a tablespoon at a time, beating at high speed or by hand until mixture is again very light and fluffy. Carefully fold flour mixture into egg mixture. Pour batter into prepared pan. Bake 13 to 15 minutes or until cake springs back when lightly touched in center. While cake bakes, generously dust a doubled strip of paper towel with powdered sugar. Loosen sides and turn out cake onto sugar-dusted towel. Trim crisp edges of cake with a sharp knife. Peel off parchment or waxed paper. Fold towel over short side of cake and roll cake and towel from short side to "set" roll as it cools. Set aside until completely cool. Unroll cooled cake and remove towel. Spread cake with jelly or jam to edges. Roll up tightly. Cut in slices to serve. Makes 10 servings.

Sponge Cake

Light and absorbent, sponge cake was said to be a favorite because "it holds more coffee than the rest." Although it is traditionally baked in a pan with a thick tube in the center, it can be baked in three layers, or in an angel food cake pan.

4 eggs, separated
2/3 cup cold water
1 cup sugar
1-1/2 cups cake flour
1/4 teaspoon salt
1 teaspoon lemon extract
1 teaspoon cream of tartar

Preheat oven to 325F (165C). In a large bowl, combine egg yolks and water. Beat at high speed 5 minutes or by hand until mixture is very fluffy and pale yellow. Gradually add sugar and beat 4 minutes longer at high speed or by hand until mixture is very light and fluffy. Sift flour and salt together into a medium-sized bowl. Add to egg-yolk mixture with mixer at low speed. Blend in lemon extract. In another large bowl with clean mixer blades, beat egg whites until frothy. Add cream of tartar; beat until whites are stiff but not dry. Using a spatula, gently fold egg whites into egg-yolk mixture. Turn batter into an ungreased 10-inch tube pan or 3 round, 8- or 9-inch, cake pans. Bake 60 to 65 minutes for a tube pan or 25 to 30 minutes for layer pans or until golden and top springs back when lightly touched. Immediately invert tube pan over a funnel or bottle; let hang until completely cool. Cool layer cakes in pans on racks. Remove cooled cakes from pans. Makes 1 (10-inch) cake or 3 (8- or 9-inch) layers.

Angel Food Cake

The Pennsylvania Dutch, master bakers, are credited with being the first to bake angel food cake. The cake is made light and airy "as the angel" by all the egg whites beaten into the mixture. Tubular angel food cake pans were first made in the United States in the 1800s, presumably to allow the cake to bake evenly.

> **1 cup cake flour, sifted before measuring, or 3/4 cup**
> **all-purpose flour**
> **1-1/2 cups sugar**
> **1-3/4 cups egg whites (12 to 14 whites)**
> **2 teaspoons cream of tartar**
> **1/4 teaspoon salt**
> **1 teaspoon vanilla extract**
> **1/2 teaspoon almond extract**

Preheat oven to 375F (190C). Sift flour and 3/4 cup sugar together into a medium-sized bowl. In the large bowl of an electric mixer, beat egg whites, cream of tartar and salt until soft peaks form. Gradually add remaining 3/4 cup sugar, a tablespoon at a time, beating on high speed until stiff peaks form. Fold in vanilla and almond extract. Fold in flour mixture, 1/4 cup at a time, just until blended. Pour batter into an ungreased 10-inch tube pan. Gently cut through batter to remove large air bubbles. Bake 30 to 35 minutes or until crust is golden and cracks are dry. Immediately invert pan over a funnel or bottle; let hang until completely cool. Remove cooled cake from pan. Makes 1 (10-inch) cake.

Chiffon Cake

— ◆ —

Chiffon cake is a cross between an angel food cake and a butter-shortened cake. It was created by an American professional baker in the 1940s who used oil instead of butter for shortening.

> 2 cups all-purpose flour
> 1-1/2 cups sugar
> 1 tablespoon baking powder
> 1/2 teaspoon salt
> 1/2 cup vegetable oil
> 5 egg yolks
> 3/4 cup cold water
> 2 teaspoons vanilla extract
> 2 teaspoons grated lemon or orange peel
> 1 cup egg whites (7 to 8 whites)
> 1/2 teaspoon cream of tartar

Preheat oven to 325F (165C). In a large bowl, combine flour, sugar, baking powder and salt. Make a well in center of mixture and add oil, egg yolks, water, vanilla and lemon or orange peel. Beat with a wooden spoon until smooth. In the large bowl of an electric mixer, beat egg whites until frothy. Add cream of tartar; beat until whites are stiff but not dry. Using a spatula, gently fold egg whites into egg-yolk mixture. Pour batter into an ungreased 10-inch tube pan. Bake 55 to 65 minutes or until a wooden skewer inserted in center comes out clean. Immediately invert pan over a funnel or bottle; let hang until completely cool. Remove cooled cake from pan. Makes 1 (10-inch) cake.

Variation
Maple-Pecan Chiffon Cake: Make Chiffon Cake, above, omitting vanilla and citrus peel. Substitute 3/4 cup packed brown sugar for 3/4 cup granulated sugar. Add 2 teaspoons maple flavoring. Fold 1 cup finely chopped pecans into batter before baking.

Vanilla Butter Cake

◆

Basic butter cake is a variation of the original 1-2-3-4 cake which followed the formula, 1 cup butter, 2 cups sugar, 3 cups flour and 4 eggs. This combination made a heavy cake. Today, baking powder and milk are added to the mixture to make a moister, lighter cake. This is a simple variation of the original cake.

> 2 cups all-purpose flour
> 2 teaspoons baking powder
> 1/4 teaspoon salt
> 1/2 cup butter, softened
> 1 cup sugar
> 1 teaspoon vanilla extract
> 2 eggs
> 2/3 cup milk

Preheat oven to 375F (190C). Grease 2 round, 8- or 9-inch, cake pans, or 1 (8-inch-square) pan. In a large bowl, combine flour, baking powder, salt, butter and sugar. Mix until blended. Add vanilla, eggs and milk. Mix at high speed or by hand, scraping sides of bowl with a spatula, until batter is smooth. Turn into greased pan or pans. Bake 25 to 30 minutes for round cakes, 40 to 45 minutes for square cake, or until a wooden pick inserted in center comes out clean. Cool on a rack before frosting. Makes 2 (8- or 9-inch) layers or 1 (8-inch-square) cake.

Seven-Minute Frosting

◆

This is a favorite for a layer cake.

> 1 egg white
> 3 tablespoons water
> 1/8 teaspoon cream of tartar
> 3/4 cup sugar
> Dash of salt

In the top of a double boiler, combine all ingredients. Stir to blend. Set aside 15 minutes or until sugar has dissolved. Place over boiling water and beat at high speed with a hand electric mixer until mixture stands in peaks. This will take about 7 minutes. Remove from heat and stir. Makes about 2-1/2 cups or enough for a 2-layer cake.

Old-Fashioned Caramel Frosting

This is a favorite for a square cake.

1 cup packed brown sugar
2/3 cup whipping cream
1 to 1-1/2 cups powdered sugar
1 teaspoon vanilla extract

In a medium-sized saucepan, combine brown sugar and cream. Stir and bring to a rolling boil. Boil 2 minutes, stirring constantly. Remove from heat. With a hand electric mixer, beat in powdered sugar and vanilla until mixture becomes thick and loses its sheen. Makes about 2-1/2 cups or enough for a 2-layer cake.

Cocoa Devil's Food Cake

— ◆ —

"To have your cake and eat it, too" might be the devilishly dark, rich, immoral, temptation of this cake. Devil's food is an American invention, and first appeared in print in the early 1900s.

2/3 cup softened butter or vegetable shortening
1-1/2 cups sugar
3 eggs
1/2 cup dark unsweetened cocoa powder
1/2 cup water
2 cups all-purpose flour
1 teaspoon baking soda
1/2 teaspoon salt
3/4 cup buttermilk
1 teaspoon vanilla extract

Grease and dust with cocoa powder 2 round, 9-inch, cake pans or 1 (13" x 9") baking pan. Preheat oven to 350F (175C). In a large bowl, beat butter or shortening and sugar at high speed or by hand until smooth and light. Beat in eggs until light and fluffy. In a cup, blend 1/2 cup cocoa powder and water. Sift flour, baking soda and salt together into a medium-sized bowl. Add cocoa mixture to egg mixture. Gently blend in flour mixture. Add buttermilk and vanilla. Pour batter into prepared pan or pans. Bake 30 to 35 minutes for round cakes, 45 to 55 minutes for oblong cake, or until a wooden pick inserted in center comes out clean. Cool on a rack before frosting. Makes 2 (9-inch) layers or 1 (13" x 9") cake.

Basic Butter Frosting

— ◆ —

Use vegetable shortening if you want a pure white frosting or one that can be colored with food coloring for decorating.

1/3 cup softened butter or vegetable shortening
3 cups powdered sugar
About 3 tablespoons whipping cream
1-1/2 teaspoons vanilla extract

In a small bowl, beat butter or shortening, powdered sugar and cream until smooth and light, adding more cream if necessary. Blend in vanilla. Mix until smooth. Makes about 2 cups or enough for a 2-layer cake.

Variations
Chocolate Butter Frosting: Add 3 ounces melted unsweetened chocolate to Basic Butter Frosting, above.
Mocha Butter Frosting: Omit vanilla. Substitute strong black coffee for whipping cream.
Browned-Butter Frosting: Use butter and melt in a heavy skillet until browned before using. Continue with Basic Butter Frosting, above.

Dutch Chocolate-Applesauce Cake

• ◆ •

Cakes are Dutch favorites and there are an amazing variety ranging from simple crumb cakes which were half bread, half cake, to loaf cakes, to moist and sumptuous chocolate and applesauce cakes. The Dutch celebrate every important event with a cake.

> 1/2 cup butter
> 2 squares unsweetened chocolate
> 2 eggs
> 1 cup sugar
> 1 cup applesauce
> 1 teaspoon vanilla extract
> 1/2 cup pecans, chopped
> 1 cup all-purpose flour
> 1/2 teaspoon baking powder
> 1/4 teaspoon baking soda
> 1/4 teaspoon salt
> Powdered sugar

Preheat oven to 350F (175C). Grease an 8- or 9-inch-square pan. In a small bowl over hot water, melt butter and chocolate together. Cool. In a large bowl, beat eggs and sugar until smooth. Add applesauce, vanilla, pecans and chocolate mixture. In a small bowl, mix flour, baking powder, baking soda and salt. Blend into applesauce mixture; beat 1 minute. Pour into greased pan. Bake 35 to 40 minutes or until a wooden pick inserted in center comes out clean. Cool on a rack. To decorate, place a doilie on top of cooled cake and dust with powdered sugar. Carefully remove doilie. Makes 9 servings.

Gingerbread

— • ◆ • —

The original gingerbread baked in early Colonial days was quite like a cookie dough. When baking powder was first introduced it was called *salaratus* and when added to the basic gingerbread batter, it made a cake similar to the one we know today. In the early days, there were two basic types of gingerbread, referred to as "lower shelf" and "upper shelf." The difference was that the "upper shelf" gingerbread had eggs and sugar in the mixture making it a gingerbread worthy for the "carriage trade." Molasses was used as the original sweetening agent and that flavor has remained a distinctive characteristic of gingerbread to this day.

> 2-1/4 cups all-purpose flour
> 3/4 cup sugar
> 1 teaspoon baking powder
> 2 teaspoons ground cinnamon
> 1 teaspoon ground ginger
> 1/2 teaspoon *each* baking soda, salt and freshly grated nutmeg
> 1/4 teaspoon ground cloves
> 3/4 cup *each* water, vegetable oil and dark molasses
> 2 eggs
> Lemon-Butter Sauce, see below
> Whipped Cream
>
> *Lemon-Butter Sauce:*
> 1/4 cup fresh lemon juice
> 1 cup sugar
> 1/2 cup butter

Preheat oven to 350F (175C). Grease a 13" x 9" baking pan. In a large bowl, combine all cake ingredients. Beat at medium speed 3 minutes or by hand. Pour into greased baking pan. Bake 35 to 40 minutes or until a wooden pick inserted in center comes out clean. While cake bakes, prepare Lemon-Butter Sauce. Pour boiling sauce over hot cake immediately as you remove it from oven. Serve warm with whipped cream. Makes 12 servings.

To prepare Lemon-Butter Sauce: In a small saucepan, combine ingredients for sauce. Bring to a boil. Stir until sugar dissolves.

War Cake

This "backwoods" country cake has been known by many names: *Eggless, Milkless, Butterless Cake; Poor Man's Cake; Hill-Billy Cake;* or *Boiled Spice Cake.* The cake can be iced with Old-Fashioned Caramel Frosting, page 159, but more often the slices are simply buttered.

2 cups dark raisins
2 cups sugar
3/4 cup lard or vegetable shortening
2 cups water
2 teaspoons ground cinnamon
1/2 teaspoon freshly grated nutmeg
1/2 teaspoon ground allspice
3-1/2 cups all-purpose flour
1 teaspoon baking soda
1 teaspoon baking powder

Preheat oven to 350F (175C). Grease and flour 2 (9" x 5") loaf pans. In a medium-sized saucepan, combine raisins, sugar, lard or shortening, water and spices. Bring to a boil, stirring; boil 5 minutes. Remove from heat. Cool to room temperature. Stir in flour, baking soda and baking powder. Divide batter between prepared pans. Bake 30 to 35 minutes or until a wooden pick inserted in center comes out clean. Turn out of pans and cool on a rack. Makes 2 loaf cakes.

1839 Pork Cake

———————— • ♦ • ————————

This early American recipe is one that thrifty farm wives baked because it used salt pork which was plentiful instead of the more expensive shortenings. A fruited spice cake, it keeps fresh for months if wrapped and kept cool. The flavor, like that of a high-quality fruit cake, improves when aged.

> 1/2 pound salt pork, coarsely ground
> 1 cup boiling water
> 4 cups all-purpose flour
> 1 teaspoon baking soda
> 1/8 teaspoon salt
> 1 teaspoon *each* ground cinnamon, cloves, allspice and nutmeg
> 1 cup raisins
> 2 eggs
> 1 cup sugar
> 1 cup light molasses

Preheat oven to 300F (150C). Grease and flour 2 (9″ x 5″) loaf pans. Ask the butcher to grind the salt pork for you. Put pork into a large bowl and pour the water over. Let stand 15 minutes. Mix flour, baking soda, salt, cinnamon, cloves, allspice and nutmeg into pork. Blend in raisins. In a small bowl, combine eggs, sugar and molasses. Mix into raisin mixture until blended. Divide batter between prepared pans. Bake 1 hour and 15 minutes or until a wooden pick inserted in center comes out clean. Turn out of pans and cool on a rack. Makes 2 loaf cakes.

Fig-Nut Loaf Cake

Our West coast and Southwest regions produce a great variety of figs that are delicious served fresh sliced in a bowl with cream. Dried figs are available all over the country and besides being good eaten out of hand, they're delicious in baked cakes, breads and bar cookies. This is a pound cake with figs added.

3/4 cup butter, softened
3/4 cup sugar
3 eggs, room temperature
2 tablespoons grated orange peel
1-1/2 cups all-purpose flour
1 teaspoon baking powder
1/2 cup chopped dried figs
1/2 cup chopped pitted dates
1/4 cup chopped pecans or walnuts
Powdered sugar

Preheat oven to 350F (175C). In large bowl, beat butter and sugar until light and fluffy. Add eggs and beat until light. Beat in orange peel. In a small bowl, combine flour and baking powder; mix 2 tablespoons of it with figs and dates. Blend remaining flour mixture into butter mixture. Fold in fig mixture and nuts until well blended. Grease and dust with powdered sugar a 9" x 5" loaf pan. Turn batter into pan. Bake 30 to 45 minutes or until a wooden pick inserted in center comes out clean. Cool in pan about 10 minutes before turning out onto a rack. Dust cooled cake with powdered sugar. Cut into thin slices to serve. Makes 1 loaf cake.

Bohemian Potica Cake

––––––––––––––––––––– •♦• –––––––––––––––––––––

It isn't a wedding, holiday, or any kind of celebration on Minnesota's Iron Range without Potica (pronounced po-teet-sa), on the table. The slices reveal a cross section of very thinly spiraled yeast dough with a pulverized nut filling. The skill of Bohemian pastry cooks is instilled into their touch from the time they are young, for you have to see, touch and experience the act of stretching a yeast dough to a 6 feet by 4 feet rectangle of egg-membrane thinness. The dough is then carefully spread with an even layer of a rather heavy nut paste. Once this is done, it is rolled up tightly and baked.

Perhaps it is true that tradition that does not change is dead. But tradition is changing! The ingredients in this simpler-to-make adaptation are almost identical to the original, but the skill required to accomplish it is much reduced. This is a wonderful bread for the holiday table!

> 2 (1/4-ounce) packages active dry yeast (scant 2 tablespoons)
> 1/4 cup warm water (105F to 115F, 40C to 45C)
> 1 cup plus 5 tablespoons sugar
> 1/4 teaspoon salt
> 3 eggs, separated
> 1/2 cup milk
> 1 cup butter, melted, cooled
> 2-1/2 cups all-purpose flour
> 2 cups ground walnuts
> 1 teaspoon ground cinnamon
> 1/4 cup milk
> 1 tablespoon honey

In a large bowl, stir yeast into warm water. Add 2 tablespoons sugar, salt and egg yolks. Let stand 5 minutes or until mixture foams. Scald 1/2 cup milk by heating almost to boiling point. Cool to 105F to 110F (40C to 45C) or until a few drops on your wrist feel warm. Blend butter, warm milk and flour into yeast mixture. Beat until satiny. Cover dough and refrigerate 8 hours or overnight. In a medium-sized saucepan, combine nuts, cinnamon, 3 tablespoons sugar, 1/4 cup milk and honey. Heat and stir until mixture is well blended. In a large bowl, beat egg whites until stiff. Gradually add remaining 1 cup sugar, beating until mixture is stiff and meringue-like. Fold into nut mixture. Preheat oven to 350F (175C). Generously grease a 10-inch tube pan. Turn out chilled dough onto a lightly floured board. Divide into 2 parts. Roll out each part to make a 20-inch square. Spread each with half of nut filling. Roll up like a jelly roll. Place one on top of the other in greased pan. With a fork, pierce through top layers of cake. Without allowing cake to rise, bake 1 hour to 1 hour 10 minutes or until a wooden skewer inserted in center comes out clean. If cake begins to brown too much during baking, cover with foil. Cool in pan before removing. Makes 1 large cake, 16 or more servings.

Peanut-Butter Wagon Wheels

The peanut is native to South America where it has been found in prehistoric graves at Ancan, Peru along with pottery decorated with peanut designs. From there the plant was carried to Africa, and then to the United States. It wasn't of much importance until George Washington Carver promoted it as a replacement for the cotton crop destroyed by the boll weevil in the 1890s. Peanut butter was created as a health food by a St. Louis doctor who was concerned about the nutrition of children. It was promoted at the 1904 St. Louis World's Fair. Today, half the annual peanut crop goes into the making of peanut butter.

> **2-1/2 cups all-purpose flour**
> **1 teaspoon baking soda**
> **1 teaspoon baking powder**
> **1 cup butter, softened**
> **1 cup peanut butter**
> **2 cups packed brown sugar**
> **2 eggs**
> **1 teaspoon vanilla extract**
> **1 cup coarsely chopped peanuts**
> **Peanut halves (optional)**

Preheat oven to 375F (190C). Lightly grease baking sheets. In a medium-sized bowl, combine flour, baking soda and baking powder. In a large bowl, beat butter, peanut butter and brown sugar until smooth and light. Beat in eggs and vanilla until light and fluffy. Stir in flour mixture. Mix just until well blended, then stir in chopped peanuts. Refrigerate dough 30 minutes. Form into balls using 1/4 cup dough for each. Place 3 balls on each greased baking sheet. Cookies spread during baking. Using a fork dipped in water, flatten to 4-1/2 inches across. Decorate with peanut halves, if desired. Bake 10 to 12 minutes or until lightly browned. Cool 10 minutes on sheets; remove to racks to finish cooling. Makes 16 large cookies.

Chip-Chocolate Cookies

— • ◆ • —

Before chocolate pieces were on the market, homemakers cut up bars of chocolate and added the pieces to cookie dough. In 1930, Ruth Wakefield, proprietress of the Toll House Inn in Vermont, sold the idea of ready-cut-up chocolate to the Nestlé company who in turn produced chocolate pieces. The famous recipe is named after the Inn and is still printed on the product's wrapper.

The following variation starts with a chocolate-flavored dough to which chocolate pieces are added.

> **2 cups all-purpose flour**
> **1/4 cup unsweetened cocoa powder**
> **1/2 teaspoon baking soda**
> **1/4 teaspoon salt**
> **1 cup butter, softened**
> **1 cup packed brown sugar**
> **1/4 cup granulated sugar**
> **2 eggs**
> **1 teaspoon vanilla extract**
> **1 (8-ounce) semisweet chocolate bar or 1-1/2 cups semisweet**
> **chocolate pieces**
> **1 cup chopped nuts**

Preheat oven to 400F (205C). In a medium-sized bowl, combine flour, cocoa powder, baking soda and salt. In a large bowl, beat butter, brown sugar, granulated sugar, eggs and vanilla until light and fluffy. Gradually stir in flour mixture; mix well. If using a chocolate bar, chip chocolate by holding bar on edge and slicing it down into 1/4-inch pieces. Stir chocolate pieces and nuts into dough. Drop by rounded teaspoonfuls onto ungreased baking sheets. Bake 8 to 10 minutes or until cookies feel firm when touched. Cool on a rack. Makes about 72 cookies.

Brownies

One type of brownie is a cross between a confection and a cake and the other is more of a cake. This is the former. Brownies are an American invention but were not published until 1897 in the Sears Roebuck Catalog.

    1 cup sugar
    2 eggs
    2 squares (2 ounces) unsweetened chocolate
    1/2 cup butter
    1/2 cup all-purpose flour
    1 teaspoon vanilla extract
    1/2 cup chopped walnuts

    Chocolate Frosting:
    1 cup sugar
    1 egg, beaten
    2 tablespoons whipping cream
    2 ounces unsweetened chocolate
    2 tablespoons butter

Preheat oven to 350F (175C). Grease an 8-inch-square pan. In a medium-sized bowl, mix sugar and eggs. In a bowl over hot water, melt chocolate and butter. Blend into egg mixture. Stir in flour, vanilla and nuts. Spread in greased pan. Bake 25 to 35 minutes or until done but still soft in center; do not overcook. Cool. Prepare Chocolate Frosting. Spread over cooled cake. Cut into 2-inch squares. Makes 16 brownies.
To prepare Chocolate Frosting: In a medium-sized heavy saucepan, combine sugar, egg, cream, chocolate and butter. Bring to a boil over medium heat, stirring constantly. Remove from heat; stir until frosting is of spreading consistency.

Amish Buttermilk Cookies

—————————— ◆ ——————————

The Amish are a rural people of Swiss-German heritage. Simple but accomplished cooks, they are good bakers and pride themselves on the great variety of their baked goods.

Legend has it that the first cookies or little *koeks* were baked as a way to test the heat of an oven. The baked dough was given to children who were the first to appreciate the special qualities of what we now know as *cookies*.

1 cup lard or softened butter
2 cups packed brown sugar
1/2 cup buttermilk
2 eggs, beaten
3-1/2 cups all-purpose flour
1 teaspoon baking powder
1 teaspoon baking soda
1/2 teaspoon salt
1 cup chopped nuts (optional)
1 teaspoon vanilla extract

Preheat oven to 350F (175C). Lightly grease baking sheets. In a medium-sized bowl, beat lard or butter and brown sugar until smooth and light. Beat in buttermilk and eggs until light and fluffy. In a medium-sized bowl, stir together flour, baking powder, baking soda, salt and nuts, if desired. Add to egg mixture; blend well. Stir in vanilla. Drop about 1/4 cup dough at a time 2 inches apart onto greased baking sheets. Bake 15 minutes or until golden. Cool on a rack. Makes about 36 large cookies.

Grandma's Ginger Crinkles

◆◆

An all-around country favorite, crinkle-topped ginger cookies are specialties of the Amish, Mennonites, Pennsylvania Dutch, Germans, Scandinavians, English, Irish and combinations of the above!

3/4 cup vegetable shortening or softened butter
1 cup packed brown sugar
1 egg
1/4 cup dark molasses
2-1/4 cups all-purpose flour
2 teaspoons baking soda
1 teaspoon ground cinnamon
1 teaspoon ground ginger
1/2 teaspoon ground cloves
1/2 teaspoon salt
Granulated sugar

Preheat oven to 350F (175C). Grease baking sheets. In a medium-sized bowl, beat shortening or butter, brown sugar, egg and molasses until light and fluffy. In a medium-sized bowl, combine flour, baking soda, cinnamon, ginger, cloves and salt. Stir into egg mixture. Shape dough into balls the size of walnuts. Roll in granulated sugar; place 2 inches apart on greased baking sheets. Bake 10 to 12 minutes or until tops of cookies feel firm; do not overbake. Cool on a rack. Makes about 48 cookies.

Spicy Oatmeal Cookies

— ◆ —

"Oatmeal" actually denotes the cooked breakfast cereal, but these cookies are made from rolled oats, meaning oats with the husks ground off then steamed and rolled flat. Iowa, Minnesota, Illinois, Wisconsin and South Dakota are the world's leading producers of oats. So let's hear it for the oat farmers!

> 1 cup butter, softened
> 1 cup packed brown sugar
> 1/2 cup granulated sugar
> 2 eggs
> 1 teaspoon baking soda
> 1/2 teaspoon salt
> 1-1/2 cups all-purpose flour
> 1 teaspoon ground cinnamon
> 3/4 teaspoon ground cloves
> 3/4 teaspoon ground ginger
> 3 cups rolled oats, quick or old-fashioned

Preheat oven to 350F (175C). In a large bowl, beat butter, brown sugar, granulated sugar and eggs until light and fluffy. Mix in remaining ingredients. Shape dough into balls the size of walnuts; place 2 inches apart on ungreased baking sheets. With a glass dipped in water, press cookies to 1/4 inch thick. Bake 8 to 10 minutes or until golden and crisp. Cool on a rack. Makes about 60 cookies.

Peg's Icebox Cookies

—◆—

These cookies were all the rage as refrigerators gained popularity. They were seen as a great convenience food because the rich dough could be made ahead and baked as time allowed. Make them when you have extra egg yolks.

> 1 cup butter, softened
> 1 cup powdered sugar
> 3 or 4 egg yolks
> 3 cups all-purpose flour
> 1 teaspoon vanilla extract

In a medium-sized bowl, beat butter, powdered sugar and egg yolks until light and fluffy. Blend in flour and vanilla until dough is stiff. Divide into 2 parts. Shape into rolls about 2 inches in diameter. Wrap in plastic wrap or foil; refrigerate until ready to use. Preheat oven to 325F (165C). Cut dough into 1/4-inch slices; place on ungreased baking sheets. Bake 8 to 10 minutes or until cookies are firm but not browned. Makes about 72 cookies.

Variations

Butterscotch Icebox Cookies: Substitute packed brown sugar for powdered sugar. Add 1 cup chopped nuts, if desired.

Chocolate Icebox Cookies: Add 2 ounces melted unsweetened chocolate to egg mixture before adding flour. Add 1 cup chopped nuts, if desired.

Oatmeal Icebox Cookies: Substitute 1-1/2 cups uncooked rolled oats for 1-1/2 cups flour.

DESSERTS

Country desserts are wholesome and uncomplicated. The delicate baked custard is basic. Stale bread or cooked rice added to the custard transformed it into a dessert that was not only "good for you" but the thrifty cook considered it a way to use up bread or rice rather than throw it out.

I never liked bread pudding. There was too much *bread* in it. But with half the bread, a few spices and "juicy" ingredients such as fresh apples and raisins added, it is a delicacy. This transformed bread pudding is served in New Orleans with a bourbon sauce. Likewise, today's rice pudding has less rice, less sugar and more seasoning.

Country cooks exemplified by the Pennsylvania Dutch, have learned to make even a simple dish of cornmeal mush taste good by using contrasts. They might eat it hot with cold milk or cold with hot milk. When they chill it, they slice and fry it, and pour old-fashioned molasses over it, or fresh comb honey, or pure maple syrup, or their own homemade, spicy apple butter.

The electric refrigerator was very expensive when it first came onto the market in the 1920s. In 1927, the General Electric Company published a cookbook of recipes and instructions for the appliance. Alice Bradley, home economist and author of the book said, "To many people electric refrigeration is still such a novelty that they scarcely realize the range of its possibilities. It is almost like having an Aladdin's lamp and not knowing the right way to rub it. . ." In her enthusiasm she described foods for the invalid, ices, sherbets and chilled desserts which the public continued to call "icebox desserts" for many years. Except for design and convenience, the basic function of the refrigerator today is the same as when it was first invented—food is kept at about 40F (5C). This not only prevents spoilage but also makes available to us an enormous range of glorious chilled desserts.

Old-Fashioned Bread Pudding

· ◆ ·

Even if there were cakes and pies, ice creams and fresh-fruit desserts, bread pudding was also on the table. Designed mainly to use up dried bread, it was never much of a treat. But with less bread and more custard, it has become an American country favorite!

1/2 (1-pound) loaf stale bread
1 quart milk (4 cups)
4 eggs
2 cups sugar
2 tablespoons vanilla extract
1 cup golden or dark raisins
2 apples, pared, cored, sliced
1/4 cup butter
Vanilla Custard Sauce, below

Preheat oven to 350F (175C). In a medium-sized bowl, crush bread into milk; mix well. In a small bowl, beat eggs. Add to bread and milk. Stir in sugar, vanilla, raisins and apples. In a small saucepan, melt butter. Pour into a 2- to 2-1/2-quart baking dish. Pour in bread mixture. Set dish in a larger baking pan; add boiling water to come halfway up sides of pudding dish. Bake 50 minutes or until pudding is set and a knife inserted near center comes out clean. Prepare Vanilla Custard Sauce. Serve cooled or warm with sauce. Makes 8 servings.

Note: Leftover cardamom coffee bread or cinnamon rolls give the bread pudding a hint of spice.

Vanilla Custard Sauce

· ◆ ·

This sauce is a dairy favorite and is excellent used not only over bread pudding but poured over fresh berries or other baked fruit desserts.

1 pint half and half or milk (2 cups)
1/4 cup sugar
4 egg yolks
2 teaspoons vanilla extract

Scald half and half or milk by heating almost to boiling point. In a medium-sized bowl, blend sugar and egg yolks. Gradually whisk hot cream or milk into yolks. Return mixture to a saucepan. Heat but do not boil. Mixture will thicken slightly. Cool. Stir in vanilla. Strain sauce into a serving pitcher or boat. If sauce curdles, process in a blender until smooth. Refrigerate until serving time. Makes 2 cups.

Creamy Rice Pudding

———————————— ◆ ————————————

Rice puddings are classic to many cuisines. This is a delicate, custardy rice pudding. To reduce calories, use a quart of milk and omit the cream. Or, it can be made with skim or two-percent milk. Bear in mind that the cream adds flavor as well as calories.

Scandinavians often serve rice pudding with a fruit soup or fruit sauce spooned over.

2/3 cup uncooked short- or medium-grain rice
2 cups water
Dash of salt
3 cups whole milk
1/2 pint whipping cream (1 cup)
1/2 cup sugar
9 egg yolks
1-1/2 teaspoons vanilla extract

Preheat oven to 300F (150C). Grease a 2-quart baking dish. In a medium-sized saucepan, combine rice, water and salt. Bring to a boil. Cook, covered, over low heat about 20 minutes or until rice has absorbed water. Scald milk and cream by heating almost to boiling point. In a medium-sized bowl, beat sugar and egg yolks. Add a little hot milk and cream to egg mixture. Whisk until smooth. Blend egg mixture with remaining milk mixture and cooked rice. Stir in vanilla. Pour into greased baking dish. Set dish in a larger baking pan; add boiling water to come 1 inch up side of dish. Bake 1 hour or until a knife inserted near center comes out clean. Serve hot, room temperature or chilled. Makes 8 servings.

Country Baked Custards

A basic custard which you can make richer by using half and half, or reduce the calories by making it with skim milk. For a custard that is more easily unmolded, add the extra egg yolks.

1 pint milk or half and half (2 cups)
1/4 cup sugar
Dash of salt
2 eggs or 2 eggs plus 2 egg yolks
1 teaspoon vanilla extract
Freshly grated nutmeg

Preheat oven to 325F (165C). Place 4 custard cups in a shallow baking pan. Scald milk or half and half by heating almost to boiling point. Stir in sugar and salt. In a medium-sized bowl, beat eggs. Gradually whisk in hot milk or half and half. Add vanilla. Strain mixture into custard cups. Sprinkle with nutmeg. Place pan with filled custard cups in oven. Pour boiling water in baking pan to come about halfway up sides of cups. Bake 30 minutes or until custards are set and a silver knife inserted off center in a custard comes out clean. Do not overbake or custards will be watery. Serve warm or chilled. Makes 4 servings.

Variations
Cream Custards: Follow directions for Country Baked Custards, above, but substitute 1 pint whipping cream for milk or half and half. Substitute 4 egg yolks for 2 whole eggs. Pour mixture into 6 tiny pot de crème cups or in heatproof demitasse cups. Set in a pan with hot water and bake as above. Makes 6 servings.
Chocolate Cream Custards: Prepare Cream Custards, above, but add 3 ounces melted semisweet chocolate to mixture. Chilled baked custard is good sprinkled with rum before serving.

Baked Cornmeal Pudding

—— • ◆ • ——

Cornmeal has always been a staple in the American diet and has been used in many ways, especially in the East and South. Indian Pudding was on the menu of the first Thanksgiving dinner. Hasty Pudding which is basically butter-fried slices of chilled, cooked cornmeal, is a classic in New England. The original cornmeal pudding was much firmer than this one. Milk poured over the top of the pudding before it is baked makes a jelly-like top layer. Serve with a special sauce or whipped cream.

> 1 pint milk (2 cups)
> 1/4 cup yellow cornmeal
> 1/2 cup light molasses
> 2 teaspoons grated gingerroot or 1 teaspoon ground ginger
> 1/2 teaspoon ground cinnamon
> 1/8 teaspoon salt
> 1 egg
> 1/2 pint cold milk (1 cup)
> Vanilla Custard Sauce, page 175, Bourbon Hard Sauce,
>   opposite, or whipped cream

Preheat oven to 300F (150C). Grease a 1-1/2-quart casserole or soufflé dish. Scald milk by heating in a medium-sized saucepan almost to boiling point. Gradually stir cornmeal into hot milk in saucepan. Cook over low heat 15 minutes, stirring, until thick. Blend in molasses, ginger, cinnamon and salt. In a small dish, whisk egg. Add a little hot cornmeal mixture to egg; whisk until blended. Blend into cornmeal mixture in saucepan. Turn entire mixture into greased dish. Let stand 15 minutes without stirring. Gently pour cold milk over top; do not mix in. Bake 1-1/2 hours or until set in center. Prepare sauce of choice or whipped cream. Serve with warm pudding. Makes 8 servings.

Bourbon Hard Sauce

—— • ◆ • ——

Bourbon is a distinctly American spirit and is made from a mash which must be at least 51 percent corn. It gets its name from Bourbon County, which was originally in Virginia, but now is part of Kentucky. Bourbon County got its name from a line of European monarchs whose subjects settled in America. According to legend, a Baptist minister, the Reverend Elijah Craig developed the distinctive flavor in 1789. The spirit was called simply *corn whiskey* or *corn*, but by the middle of the 1800s it was so much associated with Bourbon County that it became known as *bourbon*, or *Kentucky bourbon*.

1/2 cup unsalted butter, softened
1 cup packed brown sugar
4 to 5 tablespoons bourbon

In a medium-sized bowl, beat butter until light. Gradually add sugar, beating until light and fluffy. Add bourbon, a tablespoon at a time, beating until very light. Serve at room temperature. Makes about 1-1/2 cups.

Maine Cranberry Pudding

—— • ◆ • ——

Cranberry recipes have been associated with New England because the berries have been grown there since 1840. Cranberries required so much sweetening that they were not too popular in the early days when sugar was a luxury.

4 cups fresh whole cranberries, washed, dried
1-1/2 cups sugar
1/2 cup chopped walnuts
1/4 cup water
2 eggs
1 cup all-purpose flour
1/2 cup butter, melted
Vanilla ice cream

Preheat oven to 325F (165). Grease a shallow 1-1/2-quart baking dish. Spread cranberries evenly over bottom of dish. Sprinkle with 1/2 cup sugar and nuts. Pour water around berries in dish. In a medium-sized bowl, beat eggs until foamy. Add remaining 1 cup sugar, beating until light and fluffy. Fold in flour and melted butter. Spoon batter over berries. Bake 45 to 55 minutes or until pudding is golden. Serve warm with vanilla ice cream. Makes 8 servings.

Fresh-Pineapple Upside-Down Cake

When a sponge cake is baked on top of fruit, then inverted to serve, what might be called a *pandowdy* becomes an *upside-down cake*.

> 1/2 cup butter
> 3/4 cup packed light- or dark-brown sugar
> 5 to 7 slices fresh pineapple or canned pineapple slices packed
>   in natural juices, drained
> 1/4 cup chopped pecans
> 2 eggs
> 1 cup sugar
> 1/8 teaspoon salt
> 1 teaspoon vanilla extract
> 1 tablespoon butter, melted
> 1/2 cup boiling milk
> 1 cup all-purpose flour

Preheat oven to 350F (175C). In a 10- to 11-inch cast-iron skillet, melt 1/2 cup butter over low heat. Add brown sugar; blend well. Arrange pineapple and nuts over sugar in skillet; set aside. In a small bowl, beat eggs until light. Beat in sugar, salt and vanilla, continuing to beat at high speed or by hand. Combine 1 tablespoon melted butter and boiling milk. Beat into eggs until very light. On low speed or by hand, quickly beat flour into egg mixture. Pour batter into skillet, covering pineapple and nuts evenly. Bake 25 to 30 minutes or until a wooden pick inserted in cake comes out clean. Immediately invert onto a serving dish. Cut in wedges to serve. Makes 8 servings.

Strawberry Icebox Cake

—————————————— ·◆· ——————————————

In the 1920s and 1930s Americans began buying electric refrigerators which made chilled desserts a snap. When the first refrigerator appeared, the cost was about the same as buying a car! It took longer for language to change than it did for the price to come down and for some time the *fridge* was called an *icebox* as were the special desserts made in it.

The convenience of this dessert is that it can, and must, be made at least a day in advance so it can chill and set.

> 1 (10-inch) Angel Food Cake, page 156
> 1/2 cup unsalted butter, softened
> 2 cups unsifted powdered sugar
> 3 egg yolks
> 1/3 cup fresh orange juice
> 3 to 4 cups fresh strawberries
> 1 pint whipping cream (2 cups)
> 2 tablespoons powdered sugar
> 1 teaspoon vanilla extract

Cut cake crosswise into 4 equal layers. In a medium-sized bowl, beat butter and 2 cups powdered sugar until smooth and light. Beat in egg yolks and orange juice until very light and fluffy. For ease of handling, you may reassemble cake layers in tube pan in which cake was baked. Place 1 layer in bottom of pan. Spread with one-third of egg mixture. Set aside a few pretty berries for garnishing top of cake. Slice remaining strawberries. Top cake layer with about 1 cup sliced berries. Repeat layering until all 4 layers are stacked. Cover and refrigerate overnight. Or, you can wrap and freeze cake up to 1 month before serving. Before serving, remove cake from mold. In a large bowl, whip cream until stiff. Blend in 2 tablespoons powdered sugar and vanilla. Frost top and sides of cake with sweetened whipped cream. Garnish top with reserved berries. Cake may be assembled and refrigerated 4 hours before serving. Makes 12 to 16 servings.

Strawberry Shortcake

•◆•

Many Americans agree there is just one kind of strawberry shortcake, the rich biscuits that grandma made which were split and buried under bright, crushed berries, then topped with whipped cream. Cake topped with strawberries is not "Strawberry Short-cake" according to them, it is only cake topped with strawberries. Biscuits with a skimpy berry topping aren't "shortcake" either. Grandma insisted that there must be at least a quart of berries for four servings. Because this shortcake base is rich, you can make the shortcakes ahead. You can even freeze them!

> **2 cups all-purpose flour**
> **1/4 cup sugar**
> **1 tablespoon baking powder**
> **1/2 teaspoon salt**
> **1/2 cup butter**
> **2/3 to 3/4 cup milk**
> **Additional sugar**
> **6 cups fresh strawberries, quartered lengthwise**
> **1/4 to 1/2 cup sugar**
> **Slightly sweetened whipped cream**

Preheat oven to 450F (230C). In a medium-sized bowl, combine flour, 1/4 cup sugar, baking powder and salt. Using a pastry blender or 2 knives, cut in butter until it is in pea-sized pieces. With a fork, toss mixture as you add enough milk to make a moist dough. On a lightly floured board, turn out dough. Pat or roll out to 3/4 inch thick. Cut into 6 (3-inch) rounds. Place on ungreased baking sheets. Sprinkle with additional sugar. Bake 12 to 15 minutes or until golden. In a medium-sized bowl, combine berries and 1/4 to 1/2 cup sugar. To serve, split shortcakes. Spoon berries into bottom of shortcake for each serving. Place top half of cake on top of berries. Add more berries. Top with sweetened whipped cream. Makes 6 servings.

Cooked Dried-Fruit Soup or Compote

·◆·

Fruit soups or compotes are sometimes called *fruit sauce* and are served with a topping of whipped cream, heavy pouring cream or sour cream. Although they are an integral part of Scandinavian cooking, they are found in the cuisines of most cultures of the world, which are in turn, the backbone of American country cooking. For example, Finnish people serve cooked fruit soup for dessert over a creamy rice pudding. When fruits and berries are in season, the dessert is made with fresh products. In winter months, fruit soup is made by sweetening and thickening canned berries or fruit, or from dried fruits.

> 1 pound mixed dried fruit, apricots, pears, apples, pitted
>   prunes, light and dark raisins
> 2 quarts water or 1 quart *each* water and apple juice
> 1 cinnamon stick
> 3 lemon slices
> 1 cup sugar
> 2 tablespoons potato starch or cornstarch
> 1/4 cup water

Place fruit in a deep stewing kettle. Add liquid, cinnamon, lemon slices and sugar. Simmer, uncovered, 45 minutes to 1 hour or until fruit is reconstituted and tender but still firm. With a slotted spoon, remove fruit to a serving dish; discard lemon slices. In a cup, dissolve starch in 1/4 cup water. Stir into boiling liquid. Cook, stirring, 5 minutes or until thickened and clear. Pour over fruit. Serve warm. Makes 8 to 10 servings.

Variation
Fresh Berry Soup: Bring 1 quart fresh berries and 2 cups water to a boil with 3 lemon slices; omit cinnamon stick. Discard lemon slices. Mix 1/2 to 1 cup sugar with starch and 1/4 cup water. Stir into boiling mixture. Cook, stirring, 5 minutes or until thickened and clear. Makes 6 servings.

Fruit Crisp

— ◆ —

When made from apples, this is sometimes called *apple candy pie*. This same dish is also known as a *crumble* or a *brown Betty*. some say it is a brown Betty when the fruit is baked on top of the crumbs and for serving is inverted onto a serving plate. Others would call that a *pandowdy*. If this is made with cooked sliced apples, topped with crumbs, it is called *scalloped apples*.

> 5 cups prepared fruit such as berries, sliced apples, pears,
>   peaches, plums or rhubarb, singly or in combination
> 1 to 1/2 cups granulated sugar, depending on tartness of fruit
> 3 tablespoons cornstarch
> 1/2 cup fruit juice or water (less for very juicy fruits)
> 1 teaspoon ground cinnamon
> 3/4 cup all-purpose flour
> 3/4 cup packed brown sugar
> 1/2 cup butter
> Slightly sweetened, lightly whipped cream

Preheat oven to 350F (175C). Grease a shallow, 1-1/2-quart baking dish. Arrange fruit in dish. In a small bowl, mix granulated sugar and cornstarch. Sprinkle evenly over fruit. Pour juice or water evenly over fruit. In a medium-sized bowl, blend cinnamon, flour and brown sugar. With a pastry blender or 2 knives, cut in butter until crumbly. Pat crumbly mixture over fruit. Bake 30 minutes or until fruit is done and crumbs are browned. Serve warm with whipped cream. Makes 6 to 8 servings.

Fruit Grunt

♦

In New England this used to be called a *grunt*, presumably because the dumpling topping grunted as it steamed. A grunt may be called a fruit *slump* or *dumpling* or *pudding*. When the same preparation is baked rather than steamed, it is known as *cobbler* or a *buckle*.

  4 to 5 cups prepared fruit such as berries, sliced apples, pears,
     peaches, plums or rhubarb, singly or in combination
  3/4 cup sugar
  1 tablespoon cornstarch
  1 cup all-purpose flour
  2 tablespoons sugar
  1 teaspoon baking powder
  Dash of salt
  2 tablespoons softened or melted butter or vegetable
     shortening
  1/3 to 1/2 cup milk
  Whipped cream or Country-Style Ice Cream, page 193

In a heavy 2- to 3-quart pot, combine fruit, 3/4 cup sugar and cornstarch. Cover and place over low heat until fruit comes to a boil. In a large bowl, combine flour, 2 tablespoons sugar, baking powder and salt. Using a pastry blender or 2 knives, cut in butter or shortening until evenly distributed. Stir in milk, adding more if necessary to make a dough that is soft but not sticky. When fruit comes to a boil, uncover pot and drop rounded tablespoonfuls of dough onto fruit, spacing evenly. Cover tightly and simmer 15 minutes without lifting lid. Serve warm, topped with whipped cream or ice cream. Makes 6 servings.

Variation
Fruit Cobbler or Buckle: Preheat oven to 350F (175C). Combine fruit, sugar and corn-starch in a shallow 2-1/2-quart baking dish. Top with dough as above. Bake 25 to 30 minutes or until fruit mixture is thickened and topping is golden.

Pandowdy or Butter-Crusted Deep-Dish Pie

·◆·

The origin of the name "pandowdy" is a bit obscure, but seems to have something to do with the "dowdy" or unstylish appearance of the finished dessert. Sometimes this was called an *apple Jonathan*. The crust varies from a short, butter crust to one that is made like a biscuit dough. It is called a *pandowdy* when it is inverted onto a serving plate before serving. If it is served crust-side up, it is a deep-dish fruit pie, in which case it can be baked in a deep casserole or in a shallow dish.

> **2-1/2 quarts sliced, pared and cored apples, pears, peaches,**
>   **blueberries, blackberries, pitted cherries or plums**
> **1 to 1-1/2 cups sugar, depending on tartness of fruit**
> **2 teaspoons ground cinnamon**
> **1/2 teaspoon freshly grated nutmeg**
> **1/4 teaspoon salt**
> **3 tablespoons butter**
> **1-1/2 cups all-purpose flour**
> **1-1/2 tablespoons sugar**
> **2 teaspoons baking powder**
> **1/2 teaspoon salt**
> **1/2 cup chilled butter, cut into 10 pieces**
> **6 to 9 tablespoons milk**
> **1/2 pint heavy cream, whipped, lightly sweetened**

Preheat oven to 350F (175C). Turn prepared fruit into a 13" x 9" or 3-quart baking dish. In a small bowl, combine 1 to 1-1/2 cups sugar, cinnamon, nutmeg and 1/4 teaspoon salt. Sprinkle over fruit; mix to blend. Dot with 3 tablespoons butter. Sift flour, 1-1/2 table-spoons sugar, baking powder and 1/2 teaspoon salt together into a large bowl. Using a pastry blender or 2 knives, cut in 1/2 cup butter until mixture resembles coarse meal. Sprinkle with 6 tablespoons milk and toss with a fork. Add more milk to make a soft dough, if necessary. On a lightly floured board, roll out dough 1 inch larger than baking dish. Lay dough over fruit. Flute and pinch dough to edge of dish with your fingers. Bake 40 to 45 minutes or until crust is golden and fruit mixture is soft and bubbly. Serve warm or at room temperature with sweetened whipped cream. Makes 12 servings.

Basic Foolproof Lard Crust

· ◆ ·

The additions of an egg and a little vinegar make this an indestructable pastry which can stand all kinds of abuse and still bake up light and flaky!

> **2 cups all-purpose flour**
> **1 teaspoon salt**
> **2/3 cup lard or vegetable shortening**
> **1 tablespoon vinegar**
> **1 egg**
> **3 to 4 tablespoons ice water**

In a medium-sized bowl, combine flour and salt. Using a pastry blender or 2 knives, cut in lard or shortening until mixture resembles coarse crumbs. In a small bowl, mix vinegar, egg and 3 tablespoons ice water. Drizzle over flour mixture, tossing with a fork until dough holds together in a ball. Add more ice water, a tablespoon at a time, if necessary. Wrap and refrigerate 30 minutes before rolling out. Makes pastry for 1 (9-inch) double-crusted pie or 2 (9-inch) single-crusted pies.

To bake a single crust: Preheat oven to 400F (205C). On a lightly floured board, roll out half of pastry to fit a 9-inch pie pan. Carefully fit into pie pan. Line with foil or waxed paper; fill with pie weights. Use metal weights or uncooked dry beans. Bake 15 to 20 minutes or until edge of crust is golden. Lift out foil or paper and return weights or beans to their container. (I have used the same beans for at least 20 years! I keep them in a jar, and they have darkened throughout the years, but are still fine to use for pie weights). If necessary, you may return crust to oven for a few minutes to finish browning center.

Graham-Cracker Crust

· ◆ ·

This makes a good choice as the crust for an unbaked pie.

> **1-1/2 cups (21 squares) graham crackers, crushed**
> **1/4 cup white sugar or packed brown sugar**
> **1/3 cup butter, melted**

Preheat oven to 375F (190C). In a medium-sized bowl, combine crumbs, sugar and butter; blend well. Press firmly into bottom and up sides of a 9-inch pie pan. Bake 8 to 10 minutes or until golden. Cool. Makes 1 (9-inch) crust.

Note: You may simply chill pie crust without baking. However, baking produces a better flavor because the crust is toasted. Unbaked crusts sometimes stick to the pie pan.

"Recipeless" Fruit Pies

— ◆ —

Although my mother's recipe is just entitled "apple pie," it is the one she uses for any kind of fruit or berry in season. I asked my sister-in-law, Kathy Luoma, for her recipe while I was "borrowing" rhubarb for a rhubarb-strawberry pie. She answered, "Oh, I don't know, I just use my apple-pie recipe and substitute rhubarb and strawberries." I guess that's how most of us bake fruit pies. We start with our favorite apple-pie recipe and go from there!

> **Dough for Basic Foolproof Lard Crust, page 187**
> **1/2 to 3/4 cup sugar, depending on tartness of fruit**
> **1 to 2 teaspoons ground cinnamon (optional)**
> **1/2 teaspoon freshly grated nutmeg (optional)**
> **1/8 teaspoon salt**
> **3 to 4 tablespoons cornstarch, depending on juiciness of fruit**
> **4 cups prepared fruit**
> **2 tablespoons butter**

Prepare dough for crust. Use half to line a 9-inch pie pan. Preheat oven to 425F (220C). In a large bowl, combine sugar, seasonings, cornstarch and fruit. Turn into unbaked pie crust. Top with dots of butter. Roll out remaining dough to fit top of pie. Place over fruit. Trim and moisten edges. Crimp to seal. Make slits in top for steam to escape. Bake 45 minutes or until crust is golden. Makes 1 (9-inch) pie, 6 to 8 servings.

Variations

Apple Pie: Pare, core and slice tart apples. Fill pie and bake as above.

Blueberry, Blackberry, Red-Currant, Gooseberry, Raspberry, Strawberry or Fresh Cherry Pie: Clean berries; pit cherries. Use 1/4 cup cornstarch. Add 1 tablespoon lemon juice to fruit mixture. Fill pie and bake as above.

Rhubarb Pie: Cut fresh rhubarb into 1-inch chunks and measure. Because rhubarb is so tart, use 1 to 1-1/4 cups sugar for an all-rhubarb pie. Use 1/4 cup cornstarch. Fill pie and bake as above.

Rhubarb-Strawberry Pie: Combine half fresh rhubarb, cut into 1-inch chunks, and half strawberries, halved. Increase sugar to 1 cup. Use 1/4 cup cornstarch. Omit cinnamon and nutmeg. Add 1 tablespoon grated lemon peel to fruit mixture. Fill pie and bake as above.

American Cream Pie

—— ◆ ——

What is under the meringue? Chocolate, vanilla, banana, lemon, butterscotch, coconut? Dessert after the usual Sunday dinner of chicken, could have been a pie of any of these flavors.

> 1 (9-inch) baked Basic Foolproof Lard Crust or Graham-Cracker
>   Crust, page 187
> 1 cup plus 2 tablespoons sugar
> 1/3 cup all-purpose flour
> 1/4 teaspoon salt
> 1-3/4 cups milk, warmed
> 1 teaspoon vanilla extract
> 3 eggs, separated
> 1 tablespoon butter
> 1/2 teaspoon cream of tartar

Prepare and bake pie crust. Combine 3/4 cup sugar, flour and salt in the top of a double boiler. Blend in milk, vanilla and egg yolks. Add butter. Place over boiling water. Cook, stirring, about 7 minutes or until thickened and smooth. Remove from heat. Scrape sides of pan with a rubber spatula. Cover and cool over ice water; do not stir. Turn filling into baked pie crust. Preheat oven to 400F (205C). In a large bowl, beat egg whites and cream of tartar until frothy. Add remaining 6 tablespoons sugar, a tablespoon at a time, beating until mixture forms stiff peaks. Spread meringue over hot filling, sealing to edge of crust to prevent shrinking and weeping. Bake 8 to 10 minutes or until meringue is lightly browned. Cool away from drafts to prevent weeping. Makes 1 (9-inch) pie, 6 to 8 servings.

Variations
Banana Cream Pie: Slice 2 to 3 bananas into baked pie crust. Cover at once with hot vanilla filling, above. Top with meringue and bake as above.
Butterscotch Pie: Substitute 3/4 cup packed dark-brown sugar for 3/4 cup of sugar in basic recipe, above. Add 1 teaspoon fresh lemon juice along with butter. Continue and bake as above.
Chocolate Cream Pie: Add 1-1/2 ounces unsweetened chocolate to milk mixture after cooking. Let stand until chocolate melts and stir to blend. Turn into baked pie crust. Top with meringue and bake as above.
Coconut Cream Pie: Fold 1 to 2 cups flaked coconut into vanilla filling, above. Turn into baked pie crust. Top with meringue and bake as above.
Lemon Meringue Pie: Use 1/2 cup fresh lemon juice and 1-1/4 cups water in place of milk in basic recipe, above. Add grated peel of 1 lemon along with butter. Continue and bake as above.

Note: Separate eggs when they are cold. Bring to room temperature before beating to gain the greatest volume.

For an extra-high meringue, use 4 egg whites and increase sugar from 6 tablespoons to 1/2 cup.

Key-Lime Pie

◆

Key limes are not the limes you buy in every supermarket. They are native to India and were introduced to Florida in the 1500s. At maturity they turn yellow. They are rather small and spherical. The juice is not green, and the authentic key-lime pie, therefore is not green, but golden. The flavor of the key lime is more sour and has a complex, more distinctive flavor than that of regular limes. Products called "key-lime" juice are occasionally available in supermarkets, but may or may not be authentic. This pie can be made with either kind of lime, but by all means, use key-lime juice if you can get it!

Sweetened condensed milk was first manufactured in 1858 by its inventor, Gail Borden. It was used to feed the troops during the Civil War. In Key West, Florida, it was the inspiration for Key-Lime Pie, making a sweet and creamy filling out of the very tart juice.

> 1 (9-inch) baked Basic Foolproof Lard Crust or Graham-Cracker
>   Crust, page 187
> 3 eggs, separated
> 1 (12-ounce) can sweetened condensed milk
> 2/3 cup key-lime juice or fresh lime juice
> 1/2 teaspoon cream of tartar
> 6 tablespoons sugar

Prepare and bake pie crust. Preheat oven to 425F (220C). In a medium-sized bowl, beat egg yolks and condensed milk. Beat in lime juice until smooth and blended. Pour mixture into baked pie crust. In a large bowl, beat egg whites and cream of tartar until frothy. Add sugar, a tablespoon at a time, beating until mixture forms stiff peaks. Spoon meringue over filling, sealing to edge of crust to prevent shrinking and weeping. Bake 5 to 7 minutes or until meringue is lightly browned. Cool before serving. Do not refrigerate but serve at room temperature. Makes 1 (9-inch) pie, 6 to 8 servings.

Spicy Pumpkin or Squash Pie

Pumpkin and squashes were among the foods introduced to the first settlers by the American Indians. Pumpkin pie was served at the Pilgrims' second Thanksgiving dinner in 1623.

> Dough for Basic Foolproof Lard Crust, page 187
> 2 cups cooked fresh or canned pumpkin or cooked, mashed,
>   yellow squash
> 3/4 cup white corn syrup
> 2 tablespoons dark molasses
> 1 teaspoon freshly grated nutmeg
> 1 teaspoon ground cinnamon
> 1/2 teaspoon freshly grated gingerroot or ground ginger
> 1/4 teaspoon salt
> 3 eggs, slightly beaten
> 1-1/2 cups half and half or whipping cream
> Whipped Cream
> Candied ginger (optional)

Prepare dough for crust. Use half to line a 9-inch pie pan. Use remaining dough to make a second pie or freeze well-wrapped several months. Preheat oven to 450F (230C). In a medium-sized bowl, mix remaining ingredients except whipped cream and candied ginger until smooth. Pour into unbaked pie crust. Bake 10 minutes; reduce oven temperature to 350F (175C) and bake 35 to 45 minutes longer or until pie is set but moves slightly in center when jiggled. Cool, then refrigerate. Serve with whipped cream and a garnish of chopped candied ginger, if desired. Makes 1 (9-inch) pie, 6 to 8 servings.

Pecan Pie

This was sometimes called *karo pie* because it included corn syrup in the mixture.

> Dough for Basic Foolproof Lard Crust, page 187
> 1/4 cup butter, softened
> 2/3 cup packed brown sugar
> 3 eggs
> 1 cup dark or light corn syrup
> 1 cup whole pecan halves
> 2 teaspoons vanilla extract
> Whipped Cream (optional)

Prepare dough for crust. Use half to line a 9-inch pie pan. Use remaining dough to make a second pie or freeze well-wrapped several months. Preheat oven to 450F (230C). In a medium-sized bowl, beat butter and brown sugar until smooth and light. Whisk in eggs. Stir in syrup, pecans and vanilla. Pour into unbaked crust. Bake 10 minutes; reduce oven temperature to 350F (175C) and bake 30 to 35 minutes longer or until pie is set. Cool. Serve with whipped cream, if desired. Makes 1 (9-inch) pie, 6 to 8 servings.

Shoo-Fly Pie

_•◆•_

This recipe proves the Pennsylvania Dutch can make a pie out of just about anything! There are similar pies in flavor and texture, such as "oatmeal pie" and "molasses pie." Since molasses was the most common sweetening ingredient of old, all of these pies contained it. There is a theory that flies are partial to molasses and have to be chased away while the cook is making this pie.

> **Dough for Basic Foolproof Lard Crust, page 187**
> 1-1/2 cups all-purpose flour
> 1/2 cup packed brown sugar
> Dash of salt
> 1/2 teaspoon ground cinnamon
> 1/8 teaspoon ground ginger
> 1/8 teaspoon ground nutmeg
> 1/4 cup butter, room temperature
> 1/2 cup light or dark molasses
> 1/2 cup boiling water
> 1/2 teaspoon baking soda

Prepare dough for crust. Use half to line an 8- or 9-inch pie pan. Use remaining dough to make a second pie or freeze well-wrapped several months. Preheat oven to 375F (190C). In a medium-sized bowl, blend flour, brown sugar, salt, cinnamon, ginger and nutmeg. Using a pastry blender or 2 knives, cut in butter until mixture resembles coarse crumbs. In another bowl, stir together molasses, boiling water, baking soda and 1-1/2 cups crumb mixture. Pour into unbaked crust. Sprinkle top with remaining crumbs. Bake 30 to 40 minutes or until crust and crumbs are golden. Makes 1 (8- or 9-inch) pie, 6 to 8 servings.

Country-Style Ice Cream

—— • ◆ • ——

The original ice cream was made from unthinned cream, which was sweetened and flavored. In our country kitchen, we always had a basic or "master" recipe for ice cream from which we were able to make a great variety of ice creams. When there was ice, we would use the hand-crank ice-cream maker or butterchurn to freeze the mixture which always seemed to taste better than ice cream from the refrigerator freezer trays. But nothing could compare with the delight of freezer ice cream in the middle of the prickly-hot days of summertime haymaking. It was in about 1940 that our farm was wired for electricity and my parents purchased an electric refrigerator, a luxury item. Along with the appliance came a cookbook that included all sorts of wondrous new possibilities. But we skipped all the mousses and such and went straight for ice cream!

Miss Alice Bradley who was the principal of Miss Farmer's School of Cookery and cooking editor of Woman's Home Companion, published in 1927 a book for the modern American homemaker called *The Electric Refrigerator Menus and Recipes*. Her basic recipe for ice cream included 27 variations in flavors, and presented a recipe that was thickened with a combination of gelatin, flour and egg to make a smooth cream.

> 6 eggs
> 1 cup sugar
> 1 pint milk (2 cups)
> 2 teaspoons vanilla extract
> 1/2 teaspoon salt
> 1 pint whipping cream (2 cups), lightly whipped

In a medium-sized bowl, beat eggs until thick and lemon-colored. Beat in sugar, milk, vanilla and salt. Fold in whipped cream. Pour into 2 freezer trays or an 8- or 9-inch-square metal pan. Freeze until partially set. Break into chunks in a large bowl. Beat with an electric mixer until light and fluffy but not melted. You may also drop the chunks, 1 at a time, through the feed tube into a food processor fitted with the steel blade and process until fluffy. Return to tray; freeze until firm. Makes 8 servings.

Variations

Maple-Nut Ice Cream: Substitute 2 teaspoons maple flavoring for vanilla. Add 1/2 cup toasted chopped pecans halfway through processing in machine or after beating.

Strawberry Ice Cream: Add 2 cups whole fresh strawberries halfway through processing in machine or during second beating; mixer will chop the berries.

Peppermint Ice Cream: Omit vanilla. Reduce sugar to 1/2 cup. Add 2/3 cup crushed peppermint-stick candies before freezing. Halfway through processing in machine or after beating, remove one-third of mixture and add a few drops of red food coloring to it. Swirl pink ice cream with white ice cream and return to machine or freezer tray.

To make Sherbets: Use only 1 cup milk. Halfway through processing in machine or at second beating, add 1 (6-ounce) can orange-juice concentrate, 1 cup red-raspberry puree, or 1 (6-ounce) can lime-juice concentrate. You may reduce sugar by half.

Note: If using a hand-crank or mechanical freezer, combine all ingredients except cream and vanilla in the top of a double boiler or in a heavy saucepan. Heat slowly, stirring, until mixture coats the back of a wooden spoon (176F, 80C). Cool. Add cream and vanilla. Turn into freezer and follow manufacturer's directions for freezing.

Ice Cream, You Scream, We All Scream for Ice Cream!

"I scream, ice cream!" was a recorded street cry of New York children in 1828. Ice cream enjoys a well-documented history and reflects many facets of American enterpreneurship which would have been impossible without the backing of the American dairy industry. What has brought wealth to the city has its foundation in the country.

It was in 1904 at the Louisiana Purchase Exposition, known as the St. Louis World's Fair, that a Syrian-American pastry maker, Ernest Hamwi heard that an ice-cream stand had run out of serving dishes. He started rolling wafer-like pastries into cornucopias as an impromptu ice-cream dish. Others later claimed they invented the ice-cream cone, but Hamwi provided the inspiration.

Ice cream itself is credited to the ancient Chinese. Marco Polo, among his many culinary souvenirs brought back to Italy a recipe for a frozen dessert based on milk. Catherine de Medicis is credited for bringing the recipe to France from Italy. In the 1700s, ice cream was being sold in the American colonies. Even George Washington possessed a "Cream Machine for Making Ice."

Thomas Jefferson, the gourmet president, introduced ice cream made with egg yolks and owned a machine he called a *sorbetière* at Monticello. Dolley Madison popularized ice cream as a dessert during her husband's term although she had helped the bachelor Jefferson with his White House parties.

It was the Italians, however, who were most involved with ice cream and were the ones to set up ice-cream shops. "Italian ice creams" or "Neapolitan ice creams" became associated with Italian immigrants.

Country folk found their own satisfactions with the popular dessert. Northerners, finding a market for their ice, shipped it to the South were it was used not only in iceboxes but for the making of ice cream. Ice cream was so available by the mid 1800s that Europeans travelling in the United States were astonished to see common laborers eating ice cream during a break.

It was in the mid-1800s that ice-cream making became mechanized. It started in 1846 when a small, compact, hand-cranked, ice-cream freezer was invented by a woman, Nancy Johnson. In 1848, a William G. Young patented the invention and began producing the "Johnson-Young Ice-Cream Maker." By 1851, a Baltimore ice-cream maker, Jacob Fussell had opened ice-cream plants in several Eastern cities and cut the price by more than half. At the same time, an associate, Perry Brazelton opened ice-cream plants in the Midwest. By the end of the 1800s, Americans were eating five million gallons of ice cream a year!

Just to paint the scenario: by 1870 Americans were eating ice cream at ice-cream parlors; by 1874 the ice-cream soda had been invented by a Robert M. Green at the Franklin Institute in Philadelphia. Milk shakes and malteds came about by the end of the century along with the sundae and by 1904 the ice-cream cone.

A Danish immigrant in Iowa made the first chocolate-covered ice-cream bar in Onawa, Iowa in 1919. He was a schoolteacher and part-time candy-store owner. He must have been a popular teacher! He called his confection the "I-Scream Bar."

BEVERAGES,
✦ CONFECTIONS & JAMS ✦

Americans have been adventurous when it comes to thirst quenchers. The tradition of tea drinking as well as the mixing of cocktails by the "genteel" is easily traced back to England. Country folk, however, figured out ways to use produce they had on hand to make a variety of beverages from rhubarb tonic, to soda beers to switchels. Mead and homemade wines made from everything from berries to dandelions to beets, potatoes and spruce and ginger were made to quench the thirst of haymakers. Honey mead hidden away in a closet for a little treat when influential friends called, or for the holiday season was potent stuff.

The name "root beer" like "ginger ale" is something of a misnomer. Root beer contains no beer. But Charles Hires, a Philadelphia pharmacist, who introduced it to the American public knew that when he named it. While honeymooning in the New Jersey countryside in the early 1870s, he found a recipe for an herb tea that consisted of 16 different wild roots and berries. When he took the beverage back to the city to market it, a friend warned him that an

herb tea wouldn't be too popular with tough Pennsylvania coal miners. So he called it *root beer*.

A hot-weather drink, still popular today was first served at the St. Louis World's fair in 1904. An innovative tea concessionaire, Richard Blechtynden, was having trouble selling his hot tea to sweltering tourists. So he dumped ice cubes into his tea and thirsty fairgoers lined up for it. It was an instant success. There are others who claimed to have invented it earlier, but this was its first public exposure.

Tea bags were invented in 1909, and although he wasn't the one who invented them, Sir Thomas Lipton was the first to market brand-name tea bags in America.

Although caffeine-free coffee isn't nearly as popular in Europe today as in our country, it was accidentally invented in 1903 by a German, Ludwig Roselius. A minor sea accident in which a shipload of coffee beans were soaked in seaweed, produced a 97 percent caffeine-free bean. With further development Roselius came up with a coffee *sans caffeine* (thus the name "sanka"), which was introduced to the American market in 1923.

It is the Pennsylvania Dutch with their tradition for "seven sweets and seven sours" that accounts for much of the variety of relishes, pickles, jams, jellies and conserves on the American table. Any fruit or vegetable that the garden offered in profusion found itself preserved in a sweet or sour or a sweet *and* sour brine. Bountiful harvests resulted in lots of recipes for the excess produce. There is hardly a country cook who can resist making a few jars of jams, jellies and marmalades from wild and tame berries and fruits.

The taste for candy dates back into ancient history and Americans have made their contributions. Fudge, peanut brittle and caramel corn are "clasic native Americans."

Shaker Mulled Cider

· ◆ ·

In the early days, neither water nor milk were used for beverages. Water was a scarce item because wells had to be dug, and they were located in the barnyard for watering the stock. It was believed that milk caused various diseases, and it probably did, since milk is a ready medium for the growth of bacteria when handled in an unsanitary way—in open wooden containers as was the mode of the day. Glass milk bottles were not invented until 1880. Tea and coffee were expensive imports and scarce on the frontier, but all sorts of herbs and barks were used, such as black birch bark, spice bark, sassafras, mint, tanzy, camomile and redwood leaves.

To make the famous Shaker cider, perfect apples were selected and placed on the grass on the north or shady side of the grain barn to mellow. When at a distance of 30 feet the fragrance could be caught, they were ready for the press. Using an ancient art, the apples were simply crushed to press the fruit's juice, which was then passed through a straw sieve into barrels. The barrels were placed in a cool cellar where, after the bung was removed, time and nature did the work. After the Shakers advocated total abstinence, they pasteurized the sweet cider rather than allowing it to ferment.

> **3 quarts apple cider**
> **1 teaspoon whole cloves**
> **1 whole nutmeg**
> **1 cinnamon stick**
> **1/2 cup sugar**

Combine all ingredients in a large enamelled pot and simmer 5 minutes. Strain and serve very hot in warmed noggins (goblets). Makes 20 servings.

Sister's Mint Cup

·◆·

Fresh mint, an herb that grows with abandon throughout most of the country, has been used in such drinks as the classic Mint Julep of the South, as well as in mint-flavored teas. This is a specialty of one of the Shaker sisters. A dash of salt sprinkled on the mint leaves draws out the flavor.

> **2 cups fresh mint leaves, finely chopped**
> **Dash of salt**
> **2 cups sugar**
> **2 cups water**
> **2 quarts ginger ale or Gingerade, below**
> **Mint sprigs**

Rinse mint leaves. Place in a large pottery bowl. Sprinkle with a dash of salt. In a medium-sized saucepan, bring sugar and water to a boil. Reduce heat and simmer 3 minutes. Pour boiling syrup over mint leaves. Let stand until cool; strain. Refrigerate. Add ginger ale or Gingerade before serving. Serve very cold garnished with mint sprigs. Makes 8 servings.

Gingerade

·◆·

In 1807 Dr. Phillip Physick of New England prepared for his patients carbonated waters which were supposed to contain some of the healing properties of the mineral spring water. These carbonated waters became very popular. The Shakers at North Union made charged water flavored with fruit juices which they marketed successfully. Other Shaker communities produced *sarsaparilla* and other healing waters. This beverage is the forerunner of ginger ale.

> **4 ounces fresh gingerroot**
> **4 lemons**
> **2 quarts boiling water**
> **2 cups fresh lemon juice**
> **Regular Sugar Syrup, page 199, to taste**
> **Mint sprigs**

Cut unpeeled gingerroot into 1/2-inch cubes. With a potato peeler, remove zest from lemons. Add to gingerroot in a non-aluminum bowl. Pour boiling water over ginger and lemon zest. Let stand 15 minutes; strain. When cold, add lemon juice and sugar syrup to taste; some like it sweet and some like the tang of the lemon. Dilute with cold water and chips of ice as desired. Garnish each serving with a sprig of fresh mint. Makes 8 generous servings.

Colonial Raspberry Fruit Shrub

Strawberries, blackberries or black raspberries were used in this shrub, but raspberries were the very favorite. The basic syrup for the shrub can be canned for later use.

>   2 quarts (2 pounds) fresh or thawed, frozen, unsweetened red
>   raspberries
>   1 cup fresh lemon juice
>   1-1/2 cups sugar
>   2 quarts water

Place raspberries in a wide crockery or pottery bowl; crush lightly. Pour lemon juice over. In a medium-sized saucepan, bring sugar and water to a boil; boil 3 minutes or until sugar is totally dissolved. Pour over berries and lemon juice. Let stand until cool; strain. Serve immediately over ice. Makes 8 servings.

To can fruit shrub: Heat strained mixture to boiling and pour into hot, sterilized canning jars. Cap with sterilized lids and rings. Place filled capped jars on a rack in a large canning kettle. Add boiling water until jars are covered with 2 inches of water. Simmer 30 minutes. Remove from water and cool on racks away from drafts. Label before storing. To use, pour over ice. Makes 4 quarts.

Tennessee Tea

This basic syrup will keep for 3 to 4 weeks in the refrigerator and can be used to make mint juleps, iced tea or punch.

>   12 lemons
>   4 quarts water
>   1 cup packed fresh mint leaves or 1/2 cup dried mint
>   2-1/2 cups sugar

Squeeze juice from lemons. Strain juice; set aside. Put squeezed lemons, water and mint leaves into a medium-sized non-aluminum saucepan. Heat to simmering and simmer 15 minutes; do not boil. Strain and discard mint and lemons. Add lemon juice and sugar. Store in a jar in the refrigerator. Makes about 1 gallon.

Variations
Mint Juleps: Add 1 to 2 tablespoons bourbon to 1 cup syrup. Pack julep cups with crushed ice and pour in syrup mixture.
Iced Mint Tea: Add syrup to taste to unsweetened iced tea.
Punch: Mix syrup with strong unsweetened tea and pineapple juice to taste. Serve over ice.

Herbade

· ♦ ·

Garden herbs were cultivated in early Colonial times. Many herbs were considered to be medicinal, curing all varieties of illnesses. Lemon balm, which is an herb that gives off a lemony, minty aroma was not only used in this drink. Meticulous housekeepers put sprigs of it among their table linens to prevent mustiness.

> **1/2 cup lemon balm leaves, finely chopped**
> **1/2 cup fresh mint leaves, finely chopped**
> **1/2 cup Regular Sugar Syrup, below**
> **1/2 cup fresh lemon juice**
> **1/4 cup fresh orange juice**
> **4 quarts ginger ale or Gingerade, page 197**
> **Additional whole mint leaves (optional)**

In a large bowl or pitcher, combine lemon balm, mint, sugar syrup, lemon juice and orange juice; refrigerate 1 hour. Before serving, strain and add ginger ale or Gingerade. Garnish with additional mint leaves, if desired. Makes 16 servings.

Regular Sugar Syrup

· ♦ ·

This sugar syrup was kept on hand in the kitchen cupboard to use as a sweetener for all kinds of nectars and drinks. It works well because the sugar is already dissolved and mixes easily into beverages.

> **2 cups water**
> **1 cup sugar**
> **1/2 cup light corn syrup**

In a medium-sized non-aluminum saucepan, combine water, sugar and corn syrup. Bring to a simmer. Brush down sides of pan with a dampened brush to bring down any sugar granules. Cover and simmer 5 minutes. Pour into a sterilized jar. Cover and store at room temperature. Makes about 2-1/2 cups.

Dairy-Farmer's Eggnog

———————— •◆• ————————

This isn't as sweet and rich as the store-bought eggnog. It can go into the punch bowl spiked or nay, with puffs of whipped cream and a sprinkling of nutmeg for garnish. To really shave off the calories you can make it with skim milk, but I prefer the richest, whole, golden Guernsey milk!

3 quarts milk
2-1/2 cups sugar
12 large eggs
Vanilla extract to taste
Freshly grated nutmeg to taste
Spirits or rum flavoring to taste
Whipped cream

In a large saucepan, heat 1 quart milk with sugar to simmering, stirring constantly to prevent burning. This can be heated in the microwave in a glass bowl. In a large bowl, whisk eggs. Gradually, whisk hot milk mixture into eggs, keeping mixture blended. Return to heat or microwave and add 1 quart milk. Heat to about 175F (80C) or just below simmering. Remove from heat and stir in remaining 1 quart milk. Add vanilla and nutmeg. Transfer to a gallon jar or large pitcher; refrigerate until ready to serve. It can be kept refrigerated up to 1 week. Add spirits or rum flavoring before serving. You may pour out individual servings and top with whipped cream. For a party, pour into a large, chilled, punch bowl and top with whipped cream. Makes about 1 gallon, 32 (1/2-cup) servings.

Never-Fail Fudge

This semisoft candy was first made in New England women's colleges. The word "fudge" had been used to mean *to hoax* or *cheat* and this candy was often cooked up by the girls on the night before examinations when they should have been studying. The first recipe for fudge was printed in 1896. Often the variations were named after women's colleges such as Wellesley and Vassar. Although fudge generally is made of chocolate, there are plenty of other flavors to use including maple, vanilla or peanut butter.

1/3 cup butter
4-1/2 cups sugar
1-1/2 cups or 1 (12-ounce) can evaporated milk, undiluted
1 cup marshmallow cream
1 (12-ounce) package milk-chocolate pieces
1 (12-ounce) package semisweet chocolate pieces
2 teaspoons vanilla extract
2 cups walnuts, coarsely chopped

Grease a 13" x 9" baking pan. In a large saucepan, combine butter, sugar and evaporated milk. Bring to a boil; boil 5 minutes. Remove from heat and add remaining ingredients except nuts. Beat well until smooth. Stir in nuts. Spoon into greased pan. Cool until firm. Cut into squares. Makes 5 pounds.

Maple-Nut Fudge

—— •◆• ——

Vermont and New Hampshire are known as maple-sugar country, even though maple sugar is produced all along the Canadian border, including northern Wisconsin and northern Minnesota. In February and March when alternate cold and warm weather encourages the sap in the maple trees to run, the season begins. Culinarily, ham is basted with maple syrup. Apples are baked with it. Cakes, cookies, frostings, puddings, gingerbread, sauces, muffins, custards, mousses, pie fillings and ice creams all end up being flavored with this tasty sweetening from the sugar bush. Maple syrup goes over pancakes, waffles, biscuits, french toast, corn fritters and fried slices of Hasty Pudding.

This delicious confection is made in New England with butternuts, but walnuts, black walnuts and pecans are good, too.

2 cups maple syrup
1 tablespoon light corn syrup
3/4 cup whipping cream
3/4 cup chopped nuts

Grease an 8-inch square pan. Pour maple syrup into a 2- to 3-quart saucepan. Add corn syrup and cream; bring to a boil. Boil, stirring occasionally, to soft-ball stage (238F to 240F/115C) or until a drop of the mixture in ice water makes a soft ball which does not hold its shape. Remove from heat and set in another pan of ice water or snow; stir until barely warm. Beat with a wooden spoon until thick and sugar crystallizes as in making fudge. Stir in chopped nuts. Pour into greased pan. Cool until firm. Cut into squares. Makes 64 (1-inch) squares.

Peanut-Butter Brittle

—— ·◆· ——

The addition of peanut butter to the mixture makes this a soft and chewy variation to regular crunchy peanut brittle.

1 cup dry-roasted peanuts
1 cup peanut butter, creamy or chunky
1-1/2 tablespoons butter
1 cup sugar
1/2 cup light corn syrup
1/4 cup hot water
1/2 teaspoon baking soda

Measure peanuts and set aside. In a small saucepan, combine peanut butter and butter. Heat just until warm. Stir to blend; set aside. Grease a baking sheet or marble slab and have ready. In a large saucepan, combine sugar, corn syrup and hot water. Clip a candy thermometer on edge of saucepan. Bring sugar mixture to a boil over high heat, stirring with a wooden spoon until mixture boils. Brush down sides of pan with a dampened brush while mixture boils, to prevent crystallization. Boil to the hard-crack stage (310F, 155C) or until a drop of the mixture in ice water separates into brittle threads. Remove pan from heat and immediately add baking soda, peanut-butter mixture and reserved peanuts; blend quickly. Pour out onto greased surface and stretch to as thin a layer as possible; it doesn't spread easily. While still warm, cut into 1-inch squares or break into pieces after it has cooled. Makes about 1-1/2 pounds.

Peanut Brittle

Peanut brittle has been made since around the turn of the century when sugar became inexpensive enough to be available to the general public. The price dropped because the sugar tariffs were lifted in the 1880s. Between 1880 and 1915, sugar consumption doubled.

> 1 cup sugar
> 1/2 cup light corn syrup
> 1/4 cup hot water
> 1/2 teaspoon salt
> 1 cup raw Spanish peanuts
> 1 teaspoon butter
> 1 teaspoon vanilla extract
> 3/4 teaspoon baking soda

Grease a baking sheet or marble slab and have ready. In a heavy saucepan, combine sugar, corn syrup, water and salt. Clip a candy thermometer on edge of saucepan. Bring mixture to a boil. Add peanuts. Cook until nuts snap and syrup begins to turn color. Add butter and vanilla. Boil, stirring occasionally, until mixture is amber-colored and reaches hard-crack stage (310F, 155C) or until a drop of the mixture in ice water separates into brittle threads. Remove from heat. Add baking soda. Pour immediately onto greased surface. Cool and pull out until very thin. Break into pieces. Makes about 1/2 pound.

Caramel Corn

"Peanuts, popcorn, crackerjack and jelly-apple, won'tcha buy from me?" Caramel corn, before it was named *Cracker Jack* was sold at the 1893 Chicago Exposition. "Crackerjack" was a slang term for anything that was considered excellent, and the name stuck. Here's a "crackerjack" you can make yourself. It is a little different in formulation because the original was made with molasses.

> 6 quarts popped corn
> 2 cups packed brown sugar
> 1 cup butter
> 1/2 cup light corn syrup
> 1 teaspoon baking soda

Grease 2 large jelly-roll pans. Put popcorn in a large bowl or dishpan. In a medium-sized saucepan, combine brown sugar, butter and syrup. Bring to a boil; boil 8 minutes. Remove from heat and add baking soda. Pour sugar mixture over popcorn, mixing well. Divide mixture between 2 greased pans. Bake at 200F (95C) 1 hour, stirring every 15 minutes. Makes 6 quarts.

Rhubarb Marmalade

—— ◆ ——

Rhubarb is an Asian native that was introduced to Europe in the 14th century and no doubt was packed along with the baggage of the early settlers. There is hardly a climate in our country where rhubarb does not thrive. It is one of the first of the springtime harvests. The first thing I do is to make a rhubarb pie. But when the harvest is abundant—and it usually is—we follow with stewed rhubarb served over rice pudding, and a variety of other rhubarb desserts. The straggler stems go into a rhubarb marmalade spiked with a bit of fresh ginger.

> 2 pounds sliced rhubarb (about 8 cups)
> 1/4 cup fresh orange juice
> 1/4 cup fresh lemon juice
> 2 tablespoons coarsely chopped fresh gingerroot
> 2-1/4 cups sugar
> 1 tablespoon grated orange peel
> 2 teaspoons grated lemon peel
> 2 oranges, peeled, seeded, sectioned
> 1 lemon, peeled, seeded, sectioned
> 1-1/2 cups walnut halves

In a large enamelled or stainless-steel pot, combine rhubarb, orange juice, lemon juice and ginger. Bring to a boil. Cover. Reduce heat and simmer 30 minutes or until rhubarb is soft. Stir in sugar. Bring to a boil. Boil rapidly 5 minutes, stirring constantly. Add peel and orange and lemon sections. Return to a boil, then remove from heat. Add walnuts. Pour into 6 hot sterilized 1-pint jars. Cap with sterilized lids and rings. Place filled capped jars on a rack in a large canning kettle. Add boiling water until jars are covered with 2 inches of water. Simmer 15 minutes. Remove from water and cool on racks away from drafts. Label before storing. Makes 6 (1-pint) jars.

Fresh Berry Jam

—— ◆ ——

Fresh berries make the best jam, and there is no need to use a commercial pectin.

> 4 cups sliced fresh strawberries, raspberries, blueberries,
>   gooseberries, blackberries, loganberries or other berries
> 3 cups sugar

In a large non-aluminum saucepan, combine berries and sugar. Stir and heat slowly to boiling, being careful mixture does not burn on the bottom. Clip a candy thermometer on edge of saucepan and boil until thermometer registers 215F to 218F (100C), the lower temperature producing a thinner jam. Ladle hot jam into 4 hot sterilized 1/2-pint jars. Cap with sterilized lids and rings. Place filled capped jars on a rack in a large canning kettle. Add boiling water until jars are covered with 2 inches of water. Simmer 15 minutes. Remove from water and cool on racks away from drafts. Label before storing. Makes 4 (1/2-pint) jars.

INDEX

BEATRICE OJAKANGAS is author of more than twenty cookbooks, including *The Great Scandinavian Baking Book,* recently elected to the James Beard Foundation/KitchenAid Cookbook Hall of Fame. Her books *Scandinavian Feasts, Scandinavian Cooking, The Great Holiday Baking Book, Great Old-Fashioned American Desserts, Great Whole Grain Breads, Quick Breads,* and *Pot Pies* are all published by the University of Minnesota Press. She has written for *Bon Appétit, Gourmet, Cooking Light, Cuisine,* and *Redbook* and has appeared on television's *Baking with Julia Child* and *Martha Stewart's Living.* She lives in Duluth, Minnesota.